EMOTI(
INTUITION
for Peak Performance

"Are you hot or cold? Do you react or respond? Or are you warm—a mix of both? In *Emotional Intuition for Peak Performance* be prepared to understand what it truly means to be 'hot headed' or 'cool and collected.' In order to be in the zone, we must be aware of what cognitive temperature we're operating with. Jason describes the positives of both and how a blend is optimal."

DR. BEN LYNCH, AUTHOR OF *DIRTY GENES*

"It is often the case that we focus on 'what' to do in life and not 'how' we do it. If we wish to reach the higher levels of our chosen field, then an effective methodology is going to be needed. In this book Jason Gregory expertly breaks down the psychology, spiritual elements, and practicalities of optimizing your personal potential. In doing so, what Jason has gifted to those seeking mastery in life is an invaluable guide to the 'how' of approaching any given field."

DAMO MITCHELL, AUTHOR OF *A COMPREHENSIVE GUIDE TO DAOIST NEI GONG* AND *WHITE MOON ON THE MOUNTAIN PEAK*

"*Emotional Intuition for Peak Performance* is a user's manual for optimal performance and success in anything the reader chooses to do. Herein the reader will find not only the nuts-and-bolts techniques for honing your skills, training yourself to use them for maximum efficiency, and achieving optimum performance in your chosen field but also practical applications of ancient truisms from Zen and Tao traditions that lend surprising insight into what it takes to succeed in the world today. One of this book's strongest points is that it dispels the illusion that you can eat whatever you please, ignore the need for proper exercise, and allow television and other mass media to use your mind as a dumping ground for trivial entertainment, silly advertising, fake news, and other mental garbage and still be a successful contender in your chosen field. If you wish to succeed at anything in life, you need to train and nourish both your body and your mind to deliver peak performance on demand, any time and any place, under any and all circumstances. Jason's new manual for worldly success outlines a practical program for proceeding to your goal step by step, inch by inch, and thereby realizing your dreams in life. That's a good deal for the price of a book!"

DANIEL REID, AUTHOR OF *THE TAO OF HEALTH, SEX, AND LONGEVITY* AND *THE TAO OF DETOX*

"With Jason Gregory as your guide, the reader will experience a wholesome, integral path to self-achievement. With clear language and a no-nonsense approach, Gregory shows us that living at our full optimal potential is also a path to inner peace. Harnessing the latest in cognitive science, sagely wisdom, and eastern philosophy, alongside his own wealth of personal experience, Gregory leads you through the ways of nourishing the self in our everyday lives, with creativity and intelligence. This book asks us to transform and to trust in our inmost nature, with sincerity. *Emotional Intuition for Peak Performance* is a breath of sanity much needed in our present times."

KINGSLEY L. DENNIS, PH.D., AUTHOR OF *THE SACRED REVIVAL*

"The secret to good writing is having something worthwhile to say, and Jason Gregory delivers again in *Emotional Intuition for Peak Performance*. His book is rich with ideas that are not only intellectually intriguing but compelling lessons to be applied in daily life."

DANA SAWYER, PROFESSOR OF RELIGION AND PHILOSOPHY AT THE MAINE COLLEGE OF ART

"In *Emotional Intuition for Peak Performance* Gregory helps you maximize your ability to be all of yourself, addressing the idea of peak performance but including inner peace and joy as a huge part of that. As usual, he demonstrates a wide range of knowledge and wisdom—and a nicely integrated left- and right-brained approach. An optimal life experience integrates skillful perception and action at all levels of the self, and with this book you'll find practices for every aspect of consciousness."

PENNEY PEIRCE, AUTHOR OF *TRANSPARENCY, LEAP OF PERCEPTION,* AND *FREQUENCY*

EMOTIONAL INTUITION
for Peak Performance

Secrets from the Sages
for Being in the Zone

JASON GREGORY

Inner Traditions
Rochester, Vermont

Inner Traditions
One Park Street
Rochester, Vermont 05767
www.InnerTraditions.com

Text stock is SFI certified

Cataloging-in-Publication Data for this title is available from the Library of Congress.

ISBN 978-1-62055-923-9 (print)
ISBN 978-1-62055-924-6 (ebook)

Printed and bound in the United States by Lake Book Manufacturing, Inc.
The text stock is SFI certified. The Sustainable Forestry Initiative® program
promotes sustainable forest management.

10 9 8 7 6 5 4 3 2 1

Text design and layout by Priscilla Baker
This book was typeset in Garamond Premier Pro with Optima, Suomi Sans, and
Kinesis used as display typefaces.

Because hyperlinks do not always remain viable, we are no longer including URLs
in our resources, notes, or bibliographic entries. Instead, we are providing the
name of the website where this information may be found.

To send correspondence to the author of this book, mail a first-class letter to the
author c/o Inner Traditions • Bear & Company, One Park Street, Rochester, VT
05767, and we will forward the communication, or contact the author directly at
jasongregory.org.

CONTENTS

PART 3

Optimization

ACKNOWLEDGMENTS

Emotional Intuition for Peak Performance is the culmination of seven years' work, going all the way back to 2013. Unbeknownst to me, through the process of writing other works—especially *Fasting the Mind* and *Effortless Living*—and dedicated practice of my own personal exercise regime and daily meditation, I discovered and created a book on how to cultivate skill and experience peak performance. When I first started teaching and writing about Eastern philosophy, I had no inkling that there was any connection to expert skill and peak performance. Nor did I consider how crucial understanding Eastern thought was for someone who wished to reach peak performance in their given skill. These are the sorts of mysterious paths you can end up in by leaving life's door ajar for new possibilities to enter. And in any quest for reaching peak performance, although it may seem like a solitary endeavor, there are usually a lot of people to thank in the background who go unnoticed and deserve the utmost praise.

My wife, Gayoung, is someone I cannot express enough love and gratitude to for being in my life. From the day that we met until now, our love for each other has never wavered and has only become stronger. My life with you is a joy I once thought was never possible to experience—I am joyful every day, and that is because of you. My relationship with you is the main reason my work, including all of the books that I have written, flourishes. For this book, like all of my previous books, you were instrumental in the writing and editing process, sharing very important suggestions that contributed to making the book more comprehensive. My love for you cannot be expressed in words, but I will go ahead and tell you what I tell you every day: I love you.

To Thailand, the land of smiles, I owe a lot. In the last twelve years, I have mainly resided in Thailand, especially Chiang Mai. These have been some of the greatest years of my life, as I have written most of my books here and also lived a peaceful lifestyle that only somewhere like Thailand can facilitate. The Thai people and culture have been a positive influence in my life, which has allowed me to go deeper in my work. *Emotional Intuition for Peak Performance* was written in its entirety in a small (extremely hot) apartment in Chiang Mai.

One of the most amazing things I have discovered as a writer is that somehow I found the perfect publisher for my work. Words are inadequate to describe the love and appreciation I have for all of the wonderful people at Inner Traditions • Bear & Company. It all begins with the wisest acquisition editor in the game, Jon Graham. Without you, Jon, none of my books would have had life breathed into them. You have always guided me in the right direction and taught me to be patient as an author. The body of work you have created in life has been in selfless service to others (authors), which should be praised and is something we can all learn from.

To the two editors of this book I owe a special debt of gratitude. First of all, I am extremely thankful to my copy editor, Jill Rogers. You made the editing process more fun than expected. Your humor and also praise for certain areas of the book were unexpected, but deeply appreciated and a welcome change. Your edit of this book was in line with the core philosophy of it; your emotional intuition was on point. Second, I cannot give enough heartfelt gratitude to my project editor, Meghan MacLean. You've been there from the beginning, and every book has been a joy to work on with you. There are many superlatives I should shower you with, but the most amazing thing to me is that, as with my last book, you gave birth to another wonderful child during the process of editing this one. How you can meticulously edit a book and deal with authors while being pregnant is a skill that I'm sure is hard for anyone to master. But you have, and since we are making a habit of this, I am expecting nothing different for my next book.

When I speak of Inner Traditions, we are all in debt to the founder and visionary, Ehud Sperling. Without you none of this is possible. You have given authors such as me a place to deliver deep content that the mainstream shirks its responsibility to humanity to share. You have created a library of wisdom that will live on well beyond all of our years. The future of our world is indebted to your selfless service, Ehud.

Last but definitely not least, I offer a humble bow to all of the great masters of the ancient East and also the teachers within modern science, especially in the fields of cognitive science, psychology, and health, who all contributed to deepening my understanding of how to cultivate skill and experience peak performance. With the help of those ancient masters and modern scientists, I hope to have developed a tool that will allow people to reach their full potential, not only enhancing their individual lives, but also contributing piece by piece to a better world we all deserve.

THE FORMULA FOR EXPERT SKILL AND PEAK PERFORMANCE

An optimal experience and life is not something that just happens to you through an abundance of wishful thinking; it depends on skills you have acquired that allow you to reach peak states of performance. You are required to set the conditions in your life that will swing things in your favor, and commitment and dedicated hard work are the means to achieve that end. We often recoil from hard work because we are used to other people telling us what to do in exchange for financial reward. But if you really want to excel in your life it takes blood, sweat, tears, and many failures to realize your full potential.

Many of us don't want to grit our teeth and move bravely through failures or accept creative criticism. We are such sensitive creatures. But keep in mind that anyone who has cultivated expertise in a skill and reached peak performance has accepted failures as lessons and words of criticism as necessary sound bites to refine their work. They were not deterred by failure or criticism. They moved with courage into the wilderness of the unknown with their guard temporarily down. We cannot accept our failures as lessons if we are always in self-protection mode. We have to learn to take the punches life inevitably dishes out and roll with them, within reason, of course.

Socially we are trained to seek financial security down well-trodden paths. We are supposed to exchange our time for a paltry financial gain in jobs we tolerate, at best. These jobs are endured to acquire this "security" we are trained to desire. Our safety net, as a result, becomes composed of mortgages, car loans, credit card debt, and so on. We need to realize that, if anything, this safety net of possessions that is supposed to grant security is more like a prison, which actually runs counter to our real goals in life.

It is truly a rare occurrence when someone reaches their optimal potential by following the conventionally beaten track—remaining in a job your whole life that doesn't inspire you only suppresses the latent potential within you waiting to be born. Yet you want to be clever about examining your life. You don't want to just quit your job and hope that miraculously something better will come along. Remember, no wishful thinking.

What you want is a good exit strategy that will sustain the path you choose to follow. It's ridiculous to just quit your job and hope that you will find something that gives you a sense of purpose. Find a sense of purpose first, and then strategize your exit plan into the wilderness of inspiration. However, it is no picnic when we choose to run counter to society's template of security. Just look at many world-class performers who had to continually grind away and overcome adversity to reach the levels of success they achieved. There are numerous obstacles you will have to endure and overcome. Anyone who reached greatness learned how to take the proverbial punch to the face and sometimes low blows that the world often produces to test our determination, will, and character. You really need a sense of humor, or you'll give up prematurely.

Being a highly productive successful achiever is not accomplished by someone who quits immediately at the first sign of difficulty. You have to have a healthy obsession or you won't last. Cultivating a skill, reaching peak performance, and even gaining peace of mind are by-products of a healthy obsession for whatever craft or path you choose to follow. You have to play the long game; a lot of people become successful not because they are special, but because they are the ones who stay in the game the longest. They have the ability to endure countless challenges and turn them into positive experiences.

We often make the mistake of focusing on the bright lights and achievements of a successful person's life. We are not usually privy to the hard work, numerous failures, and challenges they had to endure to achieve them. We usually see only the big bank accounts, mansions, cars, and fine clothes without realizing these material possessions are, in many instances, a by-product of someone's concerted and consistent effort to reach a high level of skill and peak performance in whatever it is they do. In fact, in a lot of cases, material possessions play second fiddle to the obsession a world-class performer has for cultivating more skill and reaching an optimal level of performance.

It is the hard work and dedication to being the best version of themselves that provides the endless drive that gets these successful people out of bed every morning (usually very early). As I mentioned, without a sense of humor you won't last. If you are still bound by the social habit of self-defense, then failure, criticism, and looking stupid in front of other people will make you shrink back into the social norms like a frightened turtle.

The best example I can give you is my own experience in becoming an author. I have never really been interested in material possessions, so it wasn't the idea of fame and fortune that led me to write. Rather, it was the actual *craft* of writing and using it to deliver deep and practical knowledge to help people learn and grow that motivated me. I don't have a Ph.D.; nor did I ever want one. The idea of four or more additional years of academic education never interested me, and going to university to become a writer and philosopher seemed antithetical to actually doing so, because the true way to become a good writer and teacher is to attend the greatest university in the world: *life*.

Since the socially accepted models of education always gave me the heebie-jeebies, I wasn't a particularly good student at school. There were a few times in high school when I was threatened with expulsion because I would question a teacher's knowledge outside of what they could recite from a textbook. Luckily for me the vice principal of my high school was the rugby coach, and I was the captain of the high school team.

Sport was the one thing that consumed my life when I was a child and teenager. Rugby league, which is the most popular game in Australia, and rugby union were what I excelled at when I was young. (Rugby union is what is typically known as "rugby"; rugby league is a faster, more exciting game and is often referred to as "the greatest game of all.") Nothing else—certainly not schoolwork—was of any interest to me.

It wasn't until I was an adult that I gained an interest in the workings of the mind and body and in the philosophy and practices that define Eastern thought. I was thirsty to truly understand what the great sages of the East knew, but I recognized that there was no Ph.D. in enlightenment, so I moved to Asia. It was there I discovered my love of writing, especially about Eastern thought and psychology and how this knowledge, both ancient and modern, impacts our lives directly.

It all started from writing random emails to friends about spiritual and political matters and about life in Asia. Those emails slowly turned into structured articles that would eventually get published by websites and magazines. I remember in my early days as a budding writer staying in a guesthouse with my wife along the Ganges River in Varanasi, India, for three dollars a day and churning out two lengthy articles (roughly ten thousand words) a week.

After two years of traveling all through Asia and learning from the Eastern spiritual traditions, my wife and I returned to Australia. Before we arrived home I had already started writing my first book. Since living costs in Australia are high, I had to take up regular work to pay the rent and got a job delivering expensive furniture. But every day after work I would be at the grindstone (my desk) writing my book and unknowingly cultivating more skill as a writer. My goal was clear, and nothing was going to stop me.

Once I finished my book, I had illusions of grandeur like any new author. I even thought about quitting my job, I was that confident. But all of the illusions I had were met by life. When I was looking for a literary agent and publisher, I was often questioned about my academic experience and platform as an author (at that time I only had a dozen articles, and they were relatively unknown). I tried to explain that there is no Ph.D. in Vedanta, classical yoga, Zen Buddhism, or Taoism, which were a few of the traditions I'd studied for over ten years, and that knowledge, and eventually wisdom, in Eastern thought is attained by adhering to the philosophy and practices that promise to deliver enlightened and virtuous people, whether they are doctors or gardeners. However, it seemed that some people in the book industry valued university degrees over the real, tangible experience of learning from people around the world (masters and students, alike) who are dedicated to individual liberation and world peace. As a result, like most new and unproved authors, I had to endure the pain of rejection after rejection to the point that I was numb to hearing a loud and clear *no*. I stopped counting rejections at one hundred, but I still felt I had to persevere.

A hundred more rejections didn't dampen my spirit, but they definitely bruised my ego. As a result, I sometimes questioned why I bothered to keep trying. But through hard work and perseverance I found a publisher. And it was not long after that that I began to lecture and teach on a regular basis. But I was not satisfied with my knowledge of Eastern thought, psychology, and culture, nor with the little I had achieved as a writer. I was hungrier than ever to gain more knowledge and become a better writer.

I wanted to return to Asia permanently to get a better understanding of the depth of mind the ancient sages of the East possessed. So after almost two years in Australia, my wife and I returned to Asia, making India our home first. This move was the single best decision of my life (ahem, next to marrying my wife, of course).

It's now six years later, and I'm writing these words in Thailand, where I currently reside. In this time I have published five books and lectured in numerous places around the world. I have spent a lot of time in ashrams, monasteries, and temples and immersed myself in the beautiful cultures of the East.

My understanding of deep knowledge, along with my skill for writing and explaining it in simple language, has improved immensely and came to me through repetition and many hours putting ink to paper. As the comedian Steve Martin once said, "Be so good they can't ignore you." I'm not saying I'm that good, but I enjoy cultivating skill and believe in the formula that this book delivers, because it has been tried and tested for thousands of years, and it *works*.

Keep in mind, though, I'm not going to bullshit you here. This is not a "You can do it!" motivational sort of book. On the contrary, it is solely focused on optimizing your life, which is not achieved by dreaming about a lot of money, but instead, through cultivating skill, reaching peak performance, and eventually finding inner peace and a sense of equanimity in the mind, all of which can only be achieved through dedication.

Real Success Is Defined by Performance-Based Achievement, Not Money

Books about reaching our full potential are usually oriented toward being financially wealthy, as if this somehow means one is truly successful in life. However, financial success, in and of itself, is empty. What I mean by this is, what is the use of financial wealth if you don't bring any value to the world? Many people incorrectly associate success with a hefty bank balance. We focus too much on being rich instead of cultivating a skill we can use to bring value to the world that in many cases can also provide us with the financial resources to continue following that path.

Imagine if, as a young man, Steve Jobs had all the financial security he needed; he was rich beyond his lifetime. Do you think we would have all the amazing Apple gizmos we have today? Probably not. Jobs's eventual financial wealth was a by-product of his *real* success, which was bringing value to the world through his genius. And his genius was the result of the years he spent cultivating a visionary skill.

The story of Steve Jobs and the Apple gadgets you use today all began in Steve's parents' garage with his talented friend and cofounder of Apple, Steve Wozniak. It didn't start with millions of dollars. Jobs couldn't have cultivated skill and reached peak performance as a visionary without years of failures and setbacks. In the end, Jobs's success was his sense of purpose as a visionary for humanity. It wasn't money. He brought value to the world and changed it forever.

The problem is that many people don't want to go through an arduous journey like Steve Jobs did, because it requires hard work and a sustained dedication to getting better at a skill. What a lot of people really want, sadly, is money. But what would they do with all that money if they didn't have a purpose in their lives? Would they simply want to buy a bunch of fancy things? If the answer is yes, then life amounts to nothing more than the accumulation of a bunch of meaningless material possessions.

Having a lot of "stuff" is not what life in general is really about, nor is it what *your* life is really about. We all have something great to share with the world if we can get out of the hypnotic suggestion to chase the almighty dollar. Don't get me wrong here; we all need money (unless you are a monk or sadhu [ascetic/holy man] who has renounced the world), and many people would like to have a bigger bank account. But my point is that if you don't know how to spend it wisely on a life you truly value, then you might be better off having less money in the hope of finding something that gives you a sense of purpose. A large bank balance and fancy things on their own are empty accomplishments; they are only attributed to success when they are the fruit of your skill and peak performance.

Many famous entrepreneurs have blurred the lines between financial wealth and real success. They have confused a lot of people with regard to what success is. A lot of them focus primarily on the financial aspect of life, which gives us no clear picture of how to reach our optimal potential. We have become accustomed to successful people attempting to motivate us with mantras such as, "You can do it," but this novice advice offers us no value and fails to provide any ideas on how to cultivate the skills necessary to actually pull it off.

Are such people really successful at what they do or are they just clever motivational speakers, hope marketers, and businesspeople? When I think of successful entrepreneurs, I think of Richard Branson, Bill Gates, and Arnold Schwarzenegger, people who brought something to the table that we could all benefit and learn from. These people don't have to get up in front of a crowd and repeat, "You can do it" a dozen times. Their actions and the person they have become from going through all the ups and downs with perseverance provide the inspiration that fuels us.

Our definition of what constitutes successful entrepreneurs, then, is blurry. They might have a podcast and get a lot of famous people on to interview but offer nothing else. We might think a motivational speaker or marketing guru has the answer for achieving optimal success, but the truth in many cases is that a lot of them prey on the insecurities and naive attitudes of good people. They offer no real transformative advice, but the money keeps ticking over for many of them because people continue to attend their events to get a quick pick-me-up.

If a quick pick-me-up is what you want, then this book is not for you. I'm interested in providing you with fundamental change using methods and a formula that will actually enable you to reach your optimal potential. I'm not interested in bullshitting you with empty promises and mantras. As spiritual teacher Sadhguru Jaggi Vasudev said, "No bull, just life."

Emotional Intuition for Peak Performance is a book about the *life* aspect of Sadhguru's phrase. We can attribute the idea of success being equal to how much money you have to the "no bull" part. In this book a really successful life is one in which the person has cultivated a skill, reached peak performance, and ultimately found inner peace. A concrete example of my point can be found in sports. For example, in the NBA there are many great basketball players with loads of money. But would we say they are all successful? Probably not, because a lot of players have not yet fulfilled their potential. Yet when we hear the name LeBron James, we have a working model of real success.

Likewise with the National Rugby League of Australia's (NRL) Johnathan Thurston. Although he is now retired, Thurston is regarded as an immortal among the NRL elite. He is regarded by many as the greatest player ever, in over one hundred years of competition. Almost everything Thurston touched turned to gold. What sets both of these champions apart from the pack? Is it money? Obviously not, considering a lot of players in their respective competitions earn as much money as or more than they do.

What sets them apart is their will to achieve greatness and, in doing so, leave a legacy. Their untiring tenacity to cultivate skill and train longer and harder than most, in the hope of reaching even higher states of peak performance, is what sets them apart. It is their ability to perform at the highest level consistently that makes them successful and in turn gives their life meaning and inspires others. That optimal experience is the feeling of being fully alive. You can't get that from money. Thurston and James have achieved that feeling from years of working on their skills. When you are fully alive through the peak performance of a skill and living a peak-performance lifestyle, then your life has meaning. As mythologist Joseph Campbell once said:

> People say that what we're all seeking is a meaning for life. I don't think that's what we're really seeking. I think that what we're seeking is an experience of being alive, so that our life experiences on the purely physical plane will have resonances with our own innermost being and reality, so that we actually feel the rapture of being alive.[1]

This book is designed for you to experience the true success of living at your full potential. It provides a formula, science, and practical method for tapping into the greatness that only people like James and Thurston usually experience.

The Formula for Peak Performance

In *Emotional Intuition for Peak Performance* I want to provide you with the philosophy, science, strategies, and tools that will help you cultivate expert skill and reach peak performance (and I hope find inner peace). In other words, to become a truly successful person. I will do this by unifying three unlikely bed fellows: cognitive science, Eastern thought, and modern health. These three seemingly unrelated fields hold the key to your optimal potential. By integrating all three we discover a working formula that explains and also helps to establish methods for tapping into your optimal potential.

In part 1 I will explain a theory in the field of cognitive science that is groundbreaking and that has been around for some time but is still relatively unknown. This theory details the precise function of our mind and also our mind in relation to our body. This is the idea of the embodied mind, which is where cognitive science corresponds to Eastern thought, especially that of ancient Chinese philosophers. Both cognitive science and Eastern thought build a solid foundation of how and why we develop ingrained skill and emotional intuition through the embodied-mind model. From both perspectives this ingrained skill we develop leads to a natural state of mind where our activities and life become effortless.

I will also go into the grit that is required to reach a peak state of performance. This includes mental fitness and a desire to go *all the way*, having basically a healthy obsession for greatness.

In part 2 I will take the embodied mind framework for understanding skill into the domain of practicality. I will examine the fundamentals for training and the discipline and strategies we need to apply to our life that will help us rig the game so we can win, so to speak. This is achieved by integrating the contemplative practices of the East and the recent discoveries in modern health. You will learn how to practice numerous forms of meditation, prioritize sleep, and explore diet and exercise methods and the fasting-the-mind lifestyle practice. All of these methods and practices will help you to better set the conditions for success in your life to blossom in your favor, which will ultimately facilitate an optimal state of being. I will also explain how cultivating intelligence and harnessing creativity are the fruits of our training.

In part 3 I focus on what being in a peak state of performance actually feels like. I explain how the experience of peak performance affects our daily lives, allowing us to live more naturally. I will explore an ancient debate between natural spontaneity and trained spontaneity through two ancient Chinese philosophers and how both relate to a level of freedom in our mind that most people have never experienced and that gives us the ability to trust our skill and actions. Everything you will learn in the following chapters will culminate toward the end of the book, when it will be up to you to integrate everything you have learned, so you can become the master you were born to be, to live your legend.

The peak performance formula, if studied and practiced sincerely, will transform your life in ways you probably cannot imagine. Theory and practice are essential if you want it to work for you. In many cases people will practice something, let's say meditation, but they don't know any of the theory and science behind how meditation transforms the mind. In this book you will find that out. This goes also for the function of the mind. If you are not actively engaged in studying your own mind, then this book will be of no use to you. If you are sincere about this life, about your life, then you need to understand the science of mind, the embodied mind. And where else to begin than right now. Are you ready to reach your peak performance? If so, turn the page, and remember: there is no bullshit ahead, so you don't have to watch where you step. Just move forward, and evolve into your peak state of being.

PART 1

Skill

1

THE EMBODIED MIND

Cultivating skill and reaching peak performance depends on how we understand the mind and body. This is not some new radical way of thinking. The primary focus of great thinkers throughout history has been on this study, especially of the mind. In both the East and West, understanding human thought and the mind's function has been a central focus. We've always been fascinated with why cultures and traditions developed, why certain religions were born to bind community, and why one person is more skillful at a particular craft than someone else.

The process of thinking—how and why we think—is at the foundation of philosophy, science, religion, and art. Numerous systems for understanding the mind have been developed over thousands of years. Some have stuck, and many have disappeared. But for as long as we can remember there has been a persistent myth pervading human civilization: mind-body dualism. This dualistic model of mind and body has become the standard template for which we study both. As a result, it is common for us to feel this split within us, and it is evident in our language and actions.

For example, we often say, "I had to drag myself out of bed this morning." This is quite a weird phrase when you think about it. Who is dragging whom out of bed? There is only you, so why do we assume there is another? We act as though the mind has to tell the body what to do, as if they are separate mechanisms. And it feels as though this is a laborious affair for the mind, like the body is some lazy brute. As a result, we have oriented our perspective toward a rational mind lugging around this completely irrational body. This view has contributed to and enhanced the mind-body dualistic myth. We have bought, hook, line, and sinker, the idea that we are these rational agents hindered by a body that has its own needs.

The Disembodied Myth

Mind-body dualism has led us to focus on and believe firmly in an *abstract rationality*, where reason trumps all. A lot of our educational, religious, and social systems are built on this model. We are trained to nourish and nurture this abstract rationality above all because this is supposedly who we are and how we get ahead in life. As a result we believe we are disembodied rational agents imprisoned within this meat suit we call a body.

This disembodied myth is a philosophical hangover from Plato down to Descartes and Kant. Philosophers such as these three propelled the dualistic model of mind and body along based on vague intuitions they had about a distinction between people who have minds and the physical world, which apparently doesn't have a mind. Their metaphysics led to a dualism between a disembodied mind and a physical world of *things*.

This is somewhat similar to the dualistic metaphysics of Patanjali, the founder of classical yoga. Patanjali believed that our true human essence is a pure awareness (Purusha in Sanskrit) that is not entangled with and actually separate from all the energy and matter of the material world (*prakriti* in Sanskrit). But the difference between Patanjali and the other philosophers is that Patanjali includes the mind as part of the material world and pure awareness as something different, which makes his metaphysics far more complicated for me to outline in just a few sentences. My point is that there were some remnants of mind-body dualism in the East but not to the degree that it took hold in the West.

In post-Enlightenment Europe and its colonies, rational thought was portrayed as the essence of human nature. Reason became something completely disconnected from the physical world around us. Our mind, and its rationality, was thought to be superior and distinct from the body and its emotions. This disembodied myth has implanted a split within us that confuses us to no end. We have bought into the disembodied model of mind without questioning its validity.

Science also has suffered from the disembodied model. Cognitive scientists in the mid-twentieth century treated the human mind as a brain in a container. Many experiments were concerned with abstract information processing, which led nowhere. It wasn't until the past few decades that cognitive science began to change its perspective.

Cognitive science is slowly moving away from the disembodied dualistic model and instead is beginning to treat human thought as fundamentally embodied. This means our thinking, even our abstract concepts, are grounded in concrete experiences that are linked to our bodily experiences through analogy and metaphor. Embodied cognition, then, as opposed to the disembodied view, ties thought inherently to feeling.

The rigid distinction between emotion and rationality is being brought into question by cognitive science, and this contributes significantly to the science of cultivating skill because cognitive scientists are starting to discover that the human brain is primarily designed for guiding action rather than representing abstract information. Yet the human brain can represent abstract information if it is required.

The embodied model of mind is not concerned with isolating these different functions, which is a hallmark of the disembodied myth. This embodied view of cognition is something radically revolutionary to the staunch proponents of reason. But though this may be new in the West, it is an ancient method in the East, which I will explain more about in chapter 2.

The rationalists in the world will probably scoff and throw their arms up in the air in disgust at the idea of embodied cognition. But no matter what you believe, cognitive science has made significant inroads in supporting the embodied model of the self. It has gained traction with a new model of science that examines, illustrates, and proves the reality of embodied cognition.

The Two Systems of Human Cognition

Cognitive science has shown through extensive research that we are not the paragons of reason we assume ourselves to be. Science is only just catching up to this perspective. Many sages, artists, philosophers, and even athletes have questioned the overuse of rationality because the actuality of their experience tells another story (and this may be why many artists and philosophers are considered strange by the general populace). Many sages from the East, for example, are often suspicious of rational people because they often think too much about *everything*.

An artist would say that being rational destroys beauty and truth. What is rational about a lot of art? Or even sports for that matter? Beauty is intrinsically in the performance; it is not something you have to think about but instead something to appreciate and be inspired by. And yet, though the embodied state of mind may be the normal perspective for sages, artists, philosophers, and athletes, cognitive science has developed a sophisticated model for understanding the mind-body integrated system. This relatively still-unknown model, if understood properly, benefits our awareness of ourselves and also explains some of the reasons behind the cultivation of skill, peak performance, and inner peace.

This model is known as the *dual process theory* and is based on two systems of cognitive function. Psychologists like to create unique terms that define them as different from the rest of the scientific community. The two systems are known as hot cognition, or System 1, and cold cognition, or System 2. This dual process model was likely introduced first by psychologist William James. The theory has since evolved through many influential psychologists. But the terms *System 1* and *System 2* were originally coined by psychologists Keith Stanovich and Richard West. In this book I will use the terms *hot cognition* and *cold cognition* primarily.

The hot system is the cognitive function that is automatic, spontaneous, fast, effortless, and mostly unconscious, and it is the primary driver of emotions. In the hot cognitive process there is no sense of voluntary control. Cold cognition, on the other hand, is the cognitive control center within our brain. The cold system is self-conscious, slow, deliberate, and effortful, and it is the part of our mind we refer to as ourselves, the "I." Cold cognition, then, is associated with the subjective experience of agency, choice, and concentration. In our growing world of rationality we have overemphasized the cold system and do not realize that both systems have their benefits and flaws. We need to understand that even though we feel as though we are these subjective agents who have conscious control, it is mainly hot cognition that is driving us.

Benefits and Flaws of Hot Cognition

Hot cognition is found in the more primal, unconscious regions of the brain. It is the older brain function that is more instinctual and linked to natural processes. For example, we don't need to learn how to satiate our hunger; we know we need food. Likewise, we know how to chew our food without any extensive training. Even children pick up the nuances of language, such as grammar, without any formal training in how to use the language.

Hot cognition allows us to perform bodily movements without having to think about it. For example, when you open and close your hand, do you have to think about it? Or can you just do it? These bodily skills relate to how the hot system attains skills without, in many cases, attempting to do so. If I ask you the question, what is 1+1, you know the answer immediately without having to think about it because you have learned it so well that it has become embodied in the hot system.

In the same fashion, we can detect hostility or excitement in the voice of a person without having to analyze their psychological state. Hot cognition also detects emotions in facial expressions and body language. Yet many people try to employ the cold system in such cases by saying, "I'm fine, don't worry about it." But the hot system *knows* for sure that their "poker face" is not fooling anybody. As a result, if we had no hot cognition and were only these rational agents, as many people believe, then we would have no way to navigate through the world. The way we move through the world efficiently is primarily the result of our naturally ingrained and mostly unconscious hot system.

We are born with innate skills that we share with other animals. We are prepared to perceive the world around us. Our fear of snakes and spiders and our ability to differentiate between objects, orient our attention, and avoid losses are innate skills that help us to naturally stay safe. Built upon innate skills is the hot function of learned association between ideas. Learned associations help glue the fabric of ideas and concepts into a common language. For example, we all agree that the capital of Japan is Tokyo. Thus we associate the specific name with the place and know that when we talk about Tokyo, we are all speaking of the same location. Society, culture, and religion depend on learned associations to function. Without them it would be difficult to communicate and understand each other properly.

Hot cognition also drives learned skills such as reading, understanding sentences, driving a car, remembering the rules of a mixed martial arts bout, and so on. These learned skills we share at varying degrees of understanding when we know the rules. Subtle nuances will define if we are just reading or actually understanding what we are reading. Nevertheless, the act of reading, for example, is a learned skill. But *understanding* what you are reading is also a hot process.

A well-trained psychologist, for example, might read a book on cognitive psychology and know exactly what is written, while to you and me it is pure gibberish—we can read it, but we won't necessarily understand what's being said. As a result, the psychologist can learn from the book and evolve, while you and I will simply put the book down and go on to something else. Expert skill, then, is the result of the hot system. The time and practice spent on a particular craft cultivates ingrained skill. The ability of NFL quarterback Tom Brady to throw a touchdown pass, of Tony Robbins to bust out a ten-hour lecture, and of Ida Haendel to play the violin is as hot a process as opening and closing our hand, for them anyway. This is expertise, where the skill has become embodied and the cold function of thinking and analyzing has temporarily shut down.

Spontaneity takes over, and as spectators we can appreciate the natural beauty of their skill. Not only does hot cognition bring naturalness and life to our movements, it also brings the peak states of a skill to the forefront of human awareness, making our world much more beautiful than if we had to think and analyze *everything* we do as something that should be rational.

And yet, although the hot system performs all of these wonderful things and much more, it does have some systematic flaws due to the evolution of culture that we need to understand. Flaws eventuate mainly because of our evolutionary urges and emotions. Our evolutionary needs were fixed a long time ago. Survival was in part based on the sugar and fat we found. The need for sugar and fat has not changed, but our circumstances have.

In Paleolithic times if we were not lucky enough to find fruit, vegetables, or animals naturally in the environment, then we would be in significant trouble. Finding adequate nutrition was a constant challenge for our primitive ancestors. As a result, we are hardwired to think sugar and fat are good for us, and they are what we need to consume no matter the quantity or quality. In our world today sugar and fat are so widely and freely available that to obtain them is no more challenging than using your legs to walk to the supermarket.

When we don't regulate this evolutionary impulse to seek sugar and fat in our modern world, we begin to indulge in both to excess, which leads to a host of negative consequences. It is the hot system that is constantly scouring the environment (and supermarket aisles) for sugar and fat. Hot cognition unconsciously goes to grab that next piece of chocolate cake even though you might be on a diet and know this is not good for your health. If I were to put a caramel sundae in front of you, for example, you would have a deep urge to devour that sundae to the point you are wearing it on your face à la George Costanza in the sitcom *Seinfeld*. For many people this would be like Chinese water torture, especially if you are on a diet. In this case the cold system is beneficial because you can decide that a caramel sundae and chocolate cake are not good for your long-term health, so you consciously refrain from eating them. If your cold cognition is lazy in making these decisions, then the hot system will take over.

Flaws within our hot cognition are also intrinsic in our emotions and sexual urges. Unconscious emotions and sexual urges conflict with our moral compass. A natural hot function is when we see or hear something beautiful, and our head naturally turns spontaneously. For example, a man might catch a stunning woman in his peripheral vision, and his head immediately turns to check her out. Though this act in itself is innocent, it might not be the best action for those of you who are married, either male or female, especially if your better half is right beside you.

Problems arise from this hot response when we go from appreciation of beauty to how can I sleep with this person. Cold cognition can help us in this case because it can monitor the hot system's response to something in the environment and consciously refrain from turning your head in that direction. A healthy, strong cold system can override the hot system, but a lazy cold system will be overridden by the hot system. For instance, although we can employ the cold system in this case, things can become complicated if we go from monitoring our natural tendency to look at the beautiful person to mentally weighing up the possibility and the potential outcomes of making an advance on that person. The latter attitude of the cold system is one of its obvious flaws, and I will speak about that shortly.

The hot system's spontaneous emotions can be beautiful, loving, and inspired, or they can be catastrophic. For example, when we express love for another it is a response to a deep feeling we have inside, and in turn we feel great joy in expressing those feelings (unless you are being clever and trying to get something from the other person, which is actually a cold function). We don't have to think about this love we have for people in our lives because it is intrinsically hot.

But our hot emotional responses can be disastrous when they are unconscious reactions. Many of us have been in a situation, for example, where a certain individual was talking too much and cutting you off in conversation. The first few times are surely tolerable, but after several times it might become annoying and ultimately frustrating. In many cases like this the actual victim becomes the perpetrator because we allow our emotions to get the better of us, which really means our hot system just did what it does without any intervention from the cold cognitive control centers. In this case, listening to this person incessantly talk and cut you off in conversation built up an emotional stock inside you that in the end didn't come out right. It became unbearable, and then one day when you couldn't take it anymore, you let them have it, and in some sense deservedly so, but this is definitely not a positive approach to the situation.

We have all surely experienced something similar to my example, and after such a reaction we feel terrible. This is where the cold system is beneficial in monitoring our emotions that are being triggered. If we remain conscious and in control of those hot emotions, then we will be free of error and will not incur any harm or blame. But don't get me wrong; I am not suggesting that you have to tolerate such people indefinitely. Sometimes the best solution is the most simple: if they continue to talk too much and speak over you, then just don't see them anymore. None of us is going to get a gold star from the universe for sucking it up and tolerating such acquaintances. In this circumstance it is best to employ the critical analysis of cold cognition to discern whether it is worth the time and effort to maintain such relationships.

Those fast, hot, emotional reactions are not only bound to individual circumstances but also come out of groupthink as well. Think about all the reactions of nations that have endured the tragedy of a terrorist attack. When a terrorist attack happens to a nation, the political leaders and media, who are both affected by their hot emotions, whip the population into such a frenzy that in some cases people are baying for blood. As we all surely know from the atrocities in the Middle East, the emotional hot system in this instance cannot be trusted without first consulting a clean, strong cold system (I say "clean" here because the cold system is designed to cut up reality into pieces of right and wrong, good and bad, and so on, and it is influenced by the hot impressions that become our cold cognitive beliefs that separate us from the rest of the world. So a *clean* cold system is not bound by a lot of beliefs). When we are emotionally driven in such circumstances, we tend to blame everybody else.

The philosopher George Ivanovich Gurdjieff's grandfather had a piece of cold system wisdom for us to consider in such emotionally charged circumstances. He told Gurdjieff that when you encounter a heavy emotion that wants to unintelligently react, sit with it for twenty-four hours, and then revisit the situation. All of that time to reflect and contemplate will invariably allow you to come up with the sanest solution.

Hot emotional responses can also be moved by something inspiring or exciting. For example, when we watch a sporting event and an athlete performs a "miracle" that changes or wins the game, usually for the team we support, we are moved, excited, and inspired by their display of brilliance. But when things aren't going our team's way, we start to overanalyze and complain about our team and the athlete who previously performed miracles. We lose sight of the fact that these things just happen. This reaction is a cold system response that does not have the intuitive understanding of hot cognition that this too will pass and the good times will return.

Cold cognition thinks too much in terms of defined conclusions, while the hot system is the function of our mind in accord with the nonlinearity of nature's process. Nature ebbs and flows, it doesn't operate in straight lines.

The emotional characteristic of hot cognition is also responsible for our tendency to act on impulse. Acting impulsively sustains modern consumerism. Marketers are depending on your impulsive behavior. The problem with this attitude is that if you act impulsively all the time you will likely become broke. Impulsive behavior, like mindless shopping or getting drunk, comes from a need to drown our real emotional problems out by trying to make ourselves feel good. Usually we feel a little empty after such behavior (and a little less flush with cash) because impulsivity is a momentary joyride.

You just can't act on impulse all the time, unless you are on a path of self-destruction. And yet many people try to defend their impulsive behavior. Sometimes our habit of acting on impulse is confused with intuition. Someone might justify their impulsive behavior by suggesting they were driven intuitively.

We assume at times that intuition is guiding our decision making, but in a lot of cases we are just being impulsive. For example, you might feel that you are "intuitively" drawn to buy a $5,000 film camera, but you have no skills in filmmaking. You might be attracted to filmmaking, but you can't become a filmmaker if you are not prepared to put in the time, effort, and sheer hard work to become one. Buying that camera would have nothing to do with intuition; instead it would simply be an impulsive act. Intuition is an entirely different beast from impulsivity. Intuition comes into play when we are perfectly calibrated to the environment. For example, people who cultivate a skill, such as artists and athletes, can trust their intuition because for them it is a hot cognitive sense of being able to skillfully read the terrain. Intuition begins to arise as naturally as their emotions, a sort of emotional intuition. "Emotional" here refers to honed instincts and intuitive feelings rather than an unconscious emotional reaction to a circumstance or a mood shift arising impulsively or in an imbalanced way.

We often make the mistake of assuming this emotional intuition of experts is a form of magic, especially when you see them achieve extraordinary feats. However, the accurate intuitions of experts result from prolonged practice, not magic. It is a kind of intelligent spontaneity that results from extreme dedication over an extended period of time (more on this in chapter 2). Political scientist, economist, computer scientist, sociologist, and psychologist Herbert Simon studied chess masters for an extended period of time. He showed that after a thousand hours of practice, a chess master begins to see the pieces on the board differently from the way you and I see them. Simon explains expert intuition in the following short statement:

> The situation has provided a cue; this cue has given the expert access to information stored in memory, and the information provides the answer. Intuition is nothing more and nothing less than recognition.[1]

Our emotional intuitiveness is a hallmark of hot cognition. As I said, those who are in the process of cultivating a skill have a more intimate relationship with intuition because it results from repetitive processes that allow a skill to evolve. For example, after ten years spent cultivating my skill as a writer, my intuition is far more familiar with the skill than it was in the beginning, when the process of writing felt disjointed and laborious.

Intuition is a term not only used within creative and performance-based work. We employ automatic reactions often throughout the day, sometimes without even realizing it. We might make a decision based on a hunch or a gut feeling and call it "intuition." When we don't understand the mind thoroughly, we easily believe that this form of intuition, a cognitive impulse, is something that is always right and magical. This belief is an illusion and something psychology has gone to great lengths to explain.

Our immediate reactions or impulses are not always right, and are surely not a form of magic; well, not to the degree we assume it to be. When we examine our mind and life we can see that this idea of intuition has often failed us. Immediate cognition even fails experts at times, which is why even they can have an off day. Woven into the fabric of the hot system are intuitive errors. For example, sometimes we are asked questions we know nothing about, but we give an answer anyway. This is obviously illogical, but we do it all the time. We trust our impulsive response without really analyzing the question. As a result we jump to conclusions far too quickly. If the question we are asked is something our cold system cannot retrieve from the hot system's memory bank, we just trust our hot intuition and run with it. We trust our immediate cognition to come up with the right answer so much that we are shocked when we are wrong.

I remember taking my mathematics exams in high school. Math was definitely not my forte, and I had no real clue how to answer a lot of exam questions (and I mean a truckload of them). But I was sure that my intuition was guiding me to the correct answer. Lo and behold, of course, I was wrong in most cases, even though I did manage a few correct responses purely by chance. The evidence of intuitive errors was discovered in my disastrous exam marks. Below is a puzzle to give you a concrete example of intuitive errors. Listen to your impulsive response rather than trying to solve it with your cold system:

> A bat and ball cost $1.10.
> The bat costs one dollar more than the ball.
> How much does the ball cost?[2]

What answer came to your mind? Of course the immediate answer is 10 cents. Though this puzzle seems easy on the surface, it is quite clever at tricking our impulsive response. It evokes an appealing immediate answer that is ultimately wrong. The answer is not 10 cents. Instead of using your hot intuition, come back into your cold analytical thinking. Our impulsive answer believes the ball costs 10 cents. If this is true then the total cost for the ball and bat together would be $1.20. Do the math: if the bat is a dollar more than the ball, and the ball costs 10 cents, then the bat alone would cost $1.10, and the total for both would be $1.20, not the correct total of $1.10. So the correct answer is not 10 cents but 5 cents. For those who answered correctly, the hot intuition answer surely came to the mind first, but you managed to resist the impulsive temptation.

People who trust the answer of 10 cents use little to no effort to examine the puzzle (which doesn't require that much time and effort), so their cold system endorses the immediate answer. People who run with this answer are often those accustomed to applying the least effort possible. And they are not alone. Studies of the bat-and-ball puzzle have been conducted in universities with thousands of students. The results are startling. At Harvard, MIT, and Princeton more than 50 percent of students gave the wrong answer, following hot intuition. The failure rate at other less selective universities was more than 80 percent. In these experiments we discover the same tendency toward little or no effort that we encountered in the puzzle. This is because cognitive effort is taxing, and we usually try to avoid it as much as possible.

Another example of hot intuition error is in the famous Müller-Lyer illusion. To demonstrate the automatic impulsive function of hot cognition look at figure 1.1.

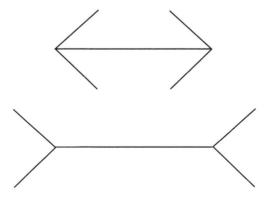

Figure 1.1. Müller-Lyer illusion

There is nothing extraordinary about the image. We see two horizontal lines of different lengths and fins on both ends pointing in different directions. The top line is shorter than the one below. Our immediate cognition believes what it sees. But are the horizontal lines really different in length? If you measure the length of both lines you discover that they are the same length. And yet, even though our cold system knows from analysis that they are the same length, our immediate cognition still perceives difference. We can train ourselves to mistrust our impulsive response, especially in regard to horizontal lines with fins attached to both ends. But remarkably, we will continue to see both lines at different lengths.

In both examples our hot cognition is seeking familiarity, not truth. The hot function perceives a pattern and trusts its hot intuition. Our hot cognition is adapted to nature and is how we navigate through nature and life with an intelligence we don't have to consciously control. But when our hot system encounters clever puzzles or visual illusions (created by the cold system), it is handicapped and rendered useless for many of us. Does any of this research imply that we are stupid? Far from it.

Psychologists believe that much of our lives are guided by the impressions coming from the hot system, so they don't believe that the people who "fail" these experiments are stupid. Instead they feel that we are guided by the impressions of the hot system even though we don't know the source of many impressions. Relying primarily on impulsivity, or hot intuition, in our daily lives is common for many of us. And as I have demonstrated, we rely on it sometimes in situations that require much slower and effortful thinking (cold system). The idea of stupidity, then, results from a weak cold system. The good news is we are not stupid.

The Benefits and Flaws of Cold Cognition

Cold cognition is a function within the prefrontal cortex (PFC), which is the cerebral cortex covering the anterior part of the frontal lobe in the brain. The PFC is a later-developing part of the brain and one aspect that defines us as different from animals. It is believed we developed the PFC as we evolved to handle environmental factors that we had to constantly navigate through. The PFC, then, is the house of the cold cognitive control functions. As I mentioned earlier, the cold system is the self-conscious, slow, deliberate, and effortful function of the mind, and also the part of our mind we refer to as "I," "me," and the seat of consciousness.

The executive control of the cold system is what stops you from reaching out for that second piece of chocolate cake or from diving head first into a caramel sundae, and as a result looking like a human sundae with it all over your face. The cold system monitors your hot inclinations and is a safeguard against unhealthy foods or foods you should avoid if you're on a diet, for example. However, if we have a weak cold system, and our cognitive controls remain lazy, we will indulge and become obese.

When we are driven primarily by hot intuition, our cold system is very weak and susceptible to the impressions of the hot system. People with a weak cold system are prone to answer questions with the first thing that comes to their mind and are unwilling to investigate their impulses. Characteristics of a weak cold system are impulsivity, impatience, and a desire for immediate gratification. These characteristics are very common in our modern world and drive consumer behavior. We are lazy drivers in the seat of our own consciousness. As a result, a lazy cold cognition will adopt suggestions coming from hot cognition.

As I demonstrated in the bat-and-ball puzzle and the Müller-Lyer illusion, hot cognition is a coherence-seeking function. When we add our coherence-seeking hot cognition to a lazy cold cognition, the cold system will endorse many beliefs based on the immediate impressions generated by the hot system. A lazy cold system, then, starts to believe it is the beliefs it endorses, and we establish an identity based on these beliefs. A weak cold system doesn't realize that beliefs are based on immediate cognitive impressions that bubble up to the surface of consciousness, which we either endorse or ignore. Beliefs change like the seasons.

A healthy mind's beliefs will continue to change and evolve. Some beliefs are good to keep (excessive sugar consumption is bad) and others aren't (my religion, God, and nation are better than everybody else's). If our cold system is weak we won't be able to discern whether these beliefs serve us or not. However, our decision making is still influenced somewhat by the hot system. The input of hot cognition never ceases. But the way to curb its influence is by strengthening your cold system.

Having a strong cold system means you have the ability to focus, strategize, and sufficiently discern between what is good or bad for you. A strong cold cognition is the hallmark of driven and successful people. Having a strong cold system is related to having a strong will as cold cognition whips our hot system into shape, much like when we have to drag ourselves out of bed in the morning. Those people with a strong will or cold cognition have the ability to push the boundaries of what we would commonly define as normal. They see their limitations as barriers, so they seek a way to hack into these limits and stretch themselves.

A musician is a great example of this kind of person. We can't just pick up an instrument and start making music. You don't bash your hands on piano keys and believe a piece by Beethoven is going to come forth beautifully.

If we ever want to play a musical instrument and have the music make sense, then we first need to learn music theory thoroughly. I have been a firsthand witness to the evolution of learning a musical instrument. My wife is a musician. As a child she played the piano and a traditional Korean instrument called a gayageum. She always had a desire to learn violin, but the circumstances of life intervened: going to university to study politics, eventually dropping out and traveling the world for years, meeting me, and then traveling the world again for years.

But in 2009 she stumbled on a cheap violin in Varanasi, India. This violin was close to being a toy, but neither one of us knew that at the time, so we bought it and found her a violin teacher in Varanasi, where we stayed for six weeks; the rest is history. She is now a competent and constantly evolving violinist, with a far better and more expensive violin. But the amount of work and dedication she has put into learning to play the violin is probably too much for those with a weak cold system (it is not uncommon for her to practice for eight hours straight). She has endured many years of cold cognitive tasks, which include becoming as adept at the language and nuances of music theory as she is at her mother tongue of Korean and, harder still, learning finger positions and how to hold the bow properly. These latter tasks are tricky because the cold system understands the theory, but it is hard for the body to adapt straight away.

Essentially, we want the study and practice of finger positions, holding the bow, and so on to become ingrained in our hot system so we can call on it on demand without having to use cold cognition to overthink it. For this to happen we need a strong cold system to prevent us from dropping the cognitively demanding task for something easier and more frivolous, such as scrolling the Facebook feed. To cultivate any skill you need to be able to focus on the task at hand. We need to pay attention to the details and embody them all. Without a strong cold system none of this is possible. But within a strong cold cognition, or any overexertion of the cold system, for that matter, we discover an inherent flaw.

The inherent flaw is that when we overemploy cold cognition, it naturally leads to a focus on rationality, which transforms us into primarily rational agents. Education and society promote this flaw. We are trained to think that if we can push and push and then push some more we will get somewhere in life and experience the social goal of financial success. Abstract rationality eventuates from a strong cold system that overanalyzes and monitors natural hot impressions.

Our whole world is in this habit because we are taught that the slow analytical thinking (cold system) is what we need to function as a human being. As a result our intelligence is based solely on our cold cognitive capabilities. A lot of people who get a high score in an IQ test have a strong cold system. But the problem with our overemphasis on our cold cognitive controls is that we forget that without the natural hot system and the impressions coming from it, cold cognition or rationality would be purely mechanical and useless. The intrinsic nature of the mind is naturally dependent on hot cognition.

People who focus on cold cognition, including people with a high IQ score, forget this fact. For example, they might be great at analyzing the details and nuances of a clever test, but they are extremely poor in emotional and social intelligence, which are intrinsically hot-system related. So someone with a strong cold cognition might be a genius but at the same time crazy because of a lack of fundamental human skills. Without fundamental human skills a genius is rendered useless and only remembered for what they were good at doing, not for who they were as a person. This is the crazy genius archetype. But these people only *appear* to be crazy because they have become victims of the disembodied myth. They regressed into reason above all, even above nature and its hot spontaneous functions.

As I mentioned earlier, cognitive science is slowly putting this disembodied myth to bed as more and more research explains that our cognition is embodied, meaning we think with our body, not our mind. But alas, strengthening your cold cognition is the primary focus in our world, and those who reach social positions of prominence, such as politicians, have strong cold systems. Coincidentally, they are judged to be fit for the position by other people with strong cold cognition.

A classic case of an overemphasis on cold cognition and reason above all else is the rise of Western intellectuals. When we tune in to many news-related programs, we invariably find a bunch of Western intellectuals sitting around debating about what is best for the world (based on their personal agendas, opinions, and cultural conditioning, of course).

A great example of this is an episode of *Real Time with Bill Maher* where actor Ben Affleck and neuroscientist Sam Harris get into a heated debate about Islam (you can watch this on YouTube*). In this episode you can see the flaws of both the hot and cold systems on dis-

---

*"Ben Affleck, Sam Harris and Bill Maher Debate Radical Islam | Real Time with Bill Maher (HBO)"

play. Host Bill Maher instigates this argument by suggesting that liberals should have a stronger stance on the Islamic world based on liberal principles. Harris chimes in with his rationality (cold cognition; he is a scientist, after all) and explains his viewpoint based on a bunch of research from poll results, which makes him believe that the Islamic world is "the mother lode of bad ideas" because from his perspective the strongest voices in the Muslim world are jihadists, and they represent a larger piece of the religion than we feel is true. His fear is that there is an underlying phenomenon of global jihadists. This statement makes Affleck erupt in emotion (hot cognition; he is an actor, after all) as he sympathizes with the Muslim world and everything they've gone through, including years of unnecessary bloodshed at the hands of Westerners. Affleck is emotionally triggered and can't believe Maher and Harris's ignorance of his point of view.

As the debate continues, Affleck becomes exhausted and dumbfounded, while Harris remains alert and poised, even though you can sense in his body language that he is either pissed off or in fear of a perceived threat and ready to get the hell out of there. Nevertheless, no matter what side of the argument you stand on, this is a classic case of hot versus cold and the flaws that define them. For instance, Affleck's unchecked emotions came out spontaneously because he had, or has, a lazy cold system. This is a situation when the cold system can benefit the hot system. Affleck could have come across much more clearly in this debate if he just breathed deeply and observed his emotions bubbling up. He could've then taken the next step wisely.

On the other hand, Harris was in far more control of his emotions (he is a cold man of reason, after all). Drawing on a lifetime of cold cognitive training, he was able to remain somewhat composed, even though his hot body language was conveying something different. But the flaw exhibited by Harris was the polar opposite of Affleck's. Harris displayed the characteristic of the disembodied myth, a rational agent caught only in his cold system without allowing some hot emotions to come out and show that he really is human. On the one hand, we can admire Harris's ability to control his emotions in such a delicate situation. On the other, if he had reduced his cold rational thinking in this debate, he might have been able to spontaneously sympathize and listen more clearly to Affleck's position and even understand why he was so emotional.

If we mainly resided in the seat of consciousness, as rational cold agents, many of us would believe that Harris came away from this argument better off because he remained somewhat composed. But the natural hot cognition within us still feels the emotions exhibited by Affleck. That sense of nature within us cannot be ignored, no matter how strong your cold cognition is. It's hard to tell what Harris's real emotions were in this argument because he was operating from the cold system. Does it mean he should've been emotionally triggered like Affleck? Of course not. But sometimes our spontaneous feelings say a lot more than a slow thinking approach that gravitates toward analysis and logic over natural feelings.

A similar phenomenon was discovered in cognitive research where you can pretend to be feeling a certain emotion, such as happiness, but deep down you are mad as hell. Our hot cognition can actually detect this in people's faces and other body language. The attempt to try to hide our real emotions is the origin of the term "poker face" in poker. Many people are clumsy at trying to hide their emotions, especially when they have either a good or bad hand in poker.

The problem for cold cognition, as I mentioned, is that our hot cognition is an aspect of nature that *knows* without thinking whether you're bullshitting or not. For instance, even though Sam Harris may have believed what he was saying, his body said something else. Maybe it was saying, "I want to kill this guy. How could he be so stupid?" But nevertheless, the body does communicate something that is covered over by a clever poker face and strong cold cognition.

From a cognitive rather than a facts-based or content standpoint, which one of them (Harris or Affleck) can be trusted? It's a hard question to answer because we focus more often on the *content* of conversations. But amazingly, even though we have primarily turned into rational agents, we still tend to trust spontaneous reactions and the immediate cognition and emotions of the hot system. This might be because, in part, we know what they're truly feeling, as you find with people who drink too much. We definitely know they're not pretending (in other words, hiding their hot emotions behind a strong cold cognition).

We also trust the natural input of the hot system in other seemingly unrelated things. For example, we prefer organic food over genetically modified organisms (GMOs) even though there is no expert conclusive scientific evidence against GMO products. But keep in mind a lot of these scientific studies on GMOs have only been measured over a short time period, so it is hard to determine long-term effects. But probably the only evidence we need to avoid GMO products concerns the weed-killing chemical glyphosate (an active ingredient in the popular herbicide Roundup). To protect the crops from the herbicide, the seeds are genetically modified to resist its effects. These seeds are known as "Roundup-ready." This means that a lot of GMO foods and some that are conventionally farmed are contaminated by glyphosate. And glyphosate is a poison far too toxic for us to consume regularly. We have a hot intuition suspicion of anything that departs from being natural; hence our concern for eating anything GMO related.

We are hardwired (hot cognition) to believe nature is good and anything artificial is bad. We tend to trust nature because the impulse to trust and nature itself are intrinsic to the hot system. Although this doesn't mean that the cold system is useless or unneeded. What it does mean is that if we overemploy the function of cold cognition to the point of disembodied rationality, we will not be trusted because we are lost in abstract rationality and ultimately have a crappy poker face.

If the hot and cold systems are not working equally to benefit each other, then we are imbalanced, and this imbalance is usually the driving force behind arguments, conflicts, and disagreements. In the case of the Affleck-Harris debate, neither individual's cognition was functioning smoothly, which is probably what caused their conflict. When we engage with *either* the untamed emotions of the hot system *or* the rationality of the cold system only, universes collide. Philosopher Jiddu Krishnamurti once said, "Conflict happens between two wrong sides, not right and wrong."

The tendency of Western intellectuals to sit around planning how they would change the world with their abstract rationality is what caused people throughout history to question reason (though they did not have the term *cold* or the knowledge of the disembodied myth). Many sages, scholars, artists, poets, and theologians have been skeptical of the function of the cold system on its own, which means they might approve more of Affleck's actions than Harris's.

Primarily cold cognitive, rational people tend to forget their innate humanness, feelings, emotions, and connection to people and nature. When we only rely on the cold system, we recoil at phenomena of the subtle or metaphysical nature. As a result science has evolved based predominantly on matter. Modern atheism is based somewhat on those same beliefs. The cold cognitive systems of science and atheism have done a good job at bashing religion, spirituality, or anything metaphysical.

The problem with the conflict between religion and science is that it is really a conflict between two functions of the brain, not different beliefs. Religion is related more to the hot system (though many religions have become rational), and science is related more to the cold system (though science is beginning to see the cognitive benefits of religion through psychology). Nevertheless, it is hard for any of us to deep down trust anybody who is functioning predominately with the cold system. As I mentioned, we are still mainly driven by the hot system, so assuming you are a rational person with complete control of yourself is erroneous.

The hot system is the source of our naturalness, and that will never change. Even though we may be able to inculcate morality, ethics, and cleverness, nature is still nature, hot cognition is still hot cognition. The organic world is primarily spontaneous, not controlled and calculated. Many sages, scholars, artists, poets, and theologians are skeptical of rationality for good reason. The all-out trust in reason should be examined. The Sufi poet Rumi explains these sentiments and in a roundabout way he explains the dance between hot and cold cognition:

Sell your cleverness and buy bewilderment;
Cleverness is mere opinion, bewilderment is intuition.
Reason is like an officer when the King appears;
The officer then loses his power and hides himself.
Reason is the shadow cast by God; God is the sun.[3]

When we are always trying to be in the effortful function of cold cognition, we tend to analyze everything as if it has a logical conclusion. This is one of the biggest illusions of reason. What is the logical conclusion of a flower? A cloud? An enjoyable evening with friends? There is no logic to define any of these. The spontaneity of life has no meaning. Children know this intuitively better than tired and learned adults.

For example, those Western intellectuals trying to know everything and change the world lose their innate innocence. They might be intelligent cold-system people, but they will never have the innocence of an Indian in rural India, for example. I am fortunate to have spent a few years in India, and while there I was overwhelmed by the rural Indians' innocence and sense of community, both of which have been lost in the developed world.

If we predominately function from the cold cognitive controls, we lose our sense of fun because everything needs to make sense. Fun does not make sense, and that is exactly why we all love it. We don't have to think about it. Fun is hot and nourishes our inner well-being and our relationships. As adults we usually lose this playfulness because we are focused on being a rational person with so-called problems we always have to attend to. Overemphasizing the function of cold cognition tempts us to believe life has meaning. But life has no real meaning. Life is life, and it is your purpose that gives life meaning for you. Having fun is likewise the same; it's a natural part of life that needs no explanation.

Why do dogs play with each other? No reason; it's just fun, and fun is the joy of spontaneity.

Wise sages throughout the course of history have been skeptical of primarily cold-system people because they have an inability to have fun and ultimately think about everything. They are far too serious. A sage's advice is to return to a childlike state of mind, which is mainly hot and embraces spontaneity. But a child still has a cold system, though it is more related to curiosity. A child will observe the movements of a snail, learn to avoid an aggressive German shepherd (I learned this one the hard way), and so on.

Children have a great sense that life is really spontaneous and not something we control. This is probably why they get frustrated with our adult rationality. What they would really want to say if they could is, "Mom and Dad, just chill out and relax." Our inability to relax is literally killing us. This firm grip on the idea of who we think we are (cold cognition) is counterproductive for our health and well-being. Even though you might be able to control your emotions and gain a big bank account, the charade can't go on forever. One thing we all discover from trying to use a lot of cold cognitive effort is that striving a lot is physiologically "expensive" (I especially feel this when I write too much in a day). We feel exhausted when we use a lot of cognitive effort. It's like we've run a marathon in our mind.

We've all experienced cognitive overload in our life, whether it was in our school days or adult working life. The result of cognitive overload in the cold system is that the hot system will eventually override the cold controls. We've all been tired or overworked and burst into fits of anger at a colleague, friend, or family member over something quite trivial. When we cool down we usually apologize by saying, "Sorry, I'm not myself today." But this is actually an inaccurate statement, considering you cannot be anybody other than yourself, unless you assume there are two people inside you. What really occurs in these situations is you lost cold cognitive control. This happens because the cold system becomes physiologically drained if overused and as a result has a limited capacity. A far more accurate apology would be, "Sorry, my cold cognition is depleted" or "Sorry, my hot cognition is just expressing its feeling of tiredness, which results from my cold system being overworked." Yet if you don't happen to know these concepts or terms, you will be speaking pure gibberish.

The cold system has a limited capacity that cannot be accessed all the time. And if you try to push those limits, it comes with disastrous consequences. When we exceed our cognitive capacity, we deplete our cold system. A depleted cold system contributes to stress, anxiety, insomnia, irritability, panic attacks, and other such mental health issues.

A good example of cognitive overload can be found in the educational system in South Korea. In high school teenagers are required to spend most of the day at school either in class or studying. Students usually arrive at school at 7:00 a.m. and leave for home at 11:00 p.m. Many students get home at midnight and study for an extra few hours. It is not uncommon for students to regularly go to sleep at 2:00 a.m. and wake up at 6:00 a.m. to do it all again. This goes on for years and has disastrous consequences.

This cognitive overload is literally killing students in South Korea. Not only are panic attacks common in South Korea (and increasingly common around the world), but teen suicide rates are one of the highest in the world. There is no time for their natural hot system to just do its thing, to be in cognitive ease and smell the roses, so to speak. What happened to kids just being kids? South Korea has embraced the disembodied myth, which runs counter to a lot of their traditional culture, and they are none the wiser for it. Even though many educational and social systems stand by this myth, it is actually counterproductive for developing skill and reaching peak performance.

Overloading our cold cognition like a South Korean student is what we believe is best for attaining success. We often think we are going to outwork the competition, but this again is disastrous and counterproductive. All we find with such overworked people and companies based on this model are a bunch of employees with depleted cold cognitions who are stressed out up to their eyeballs. This is why some workplaces can be very unfriendly environments. Depleting the cold system through cognitive overload is where the change of function transitions to the hot system.

Why do we react spontaneously in fits of anger or comments we regret when we are overworked? The answer is simply that when our cold system is depleted the hot system naturally takes over. The spontaneous hot cognitive reactions in such instances are the deep feeling of the body speaking. Hot cognition might react with, "I'm tired, stop bothering me." Or if they believe that they have more in the psychological gas tank, "Stay the fuck out of my way, I'm busy." When we hear such exhausted responses flung our way, we should be mindful that the person's cold system is depleted. But this awareness can be difficult to perceive when one is faced with the magnitude of their aggression, cynicism, sarcasm, and so on.

People who display reactions stemming from a depleted cold system are hard to trust. This is one reason the ancient sages were skeptical of the cold system. They didn't really know who they were dealing with— the deep, ingrained hot system or the guard of the cold rational agent. A sage wants to know the deep-down hot, raw material within a person rather than the strong and clever cold cognition that is playing a constant game of poker with the world.

This skeptical attitude is prevalent in Eastern thought, especially in China. The Chinese have one of the more interesting ways of doing business. When they want to conduct business with someone, instead of sitting down and going over the fine details of their business matters, they all go out and get legless drunk like you've never experienced. Are Chinese businesspeople partygoers and alcoholics? Most definitely not. Actually, this is a clever method for finding out who they're truly dealing with. Sometimes a good dose of alcoholic truth serum is all that is needed to pry into who someone truly is.

The cognitive effect of drinking downregulates* the cold system,

---

*Downregulate here refers to decreasing or lowering the strong sense of "I" ego you have within your mind, the cold cognitive function within the prefrontal cortex.

this person you refer to as "I." This allows the deep nature of the hot system to reveal itself. Chinese businesspeople obviously aren't big fans of poker faces. They want to know the genuine side of you, the authentic self. The authentic self in the East is viewed as the hot cognitive part of you and not some abstract idea of yourself upheld by the cold system. Easterners are not suggesting that the cold system is useless but rather that someone who is always trying to operate from a cold cognitive state cannot be trusted because their real intuitive beliefs can be hidden by a strong cold cognition (keep in mind that Chinese businesspeople are not using this specific terminology).

The Chinese business drinking ritual is a safeguard against any unexpected hot cognitive expressions of anger, hostility, bitterness, and so on. It should expose any of these emotions and allow companies to decide whether or not to do business with a potential client. The down-regulation of cold cognition due to excessive booze is related to how a skill is developed and made to shine. But this requires the essential aspect for cultivating a skill: the two systems have to work together.

How Hot and Cold Cognition Work Together

Earlier I mentioned learning how to play a musical instrument, and this is a good example of how both systems are required to function optimally and together to develop a skill. In music, you need to learn and understand music theory until reading music is as easy as reading your mother language. On top of this you need to learn how to manipulate your body to make the noise coming out of the instrument sound like a melody rather than a dying cat. For violin you need to train your hands to maintain certain finger positions and hold the bow. For drums you need to learn how to hold the sticks and how to hit the drums while your feet simultaneously press down on the pedals to beat the bass, or kick, drum.

Learning any musical instrument, like most things, takes time. But after a while the skill becomes embodied. The musical instrument ends up being an extension of your body, like a fifth limb, and playing it becomes as easy and unconscious as walking. It is the constant focus and repetition exercised by the cold cognition that ingrains any particular skill into our hot cognition. Once we download the cold cognitive nuances and theory of a particular skill into our hot cognition, the skill becomes spontaneous and can be accessed without having to consciously think about it. This process is constant in cultivating a skill. Psychologist Daniel Kahneman explains this cognitive phenomenon as follows:

> As you become skilled in a task, its demand for energy diminishes. Studies of the brain have shown that the pattern of activity associated with an action changes as skill increases, with fewer brain regions involved.[4]

Those dedicated to a craft will continue to develop skill. This process teaches us to disengage from our cold cognition as well, and this is really important to understand. Even though world-class performers use cold cognition to learn a certain skill, once that skill has become embodied, cold cognition is like kryptonite to the effortlessness of the hot system. For example, a musician will perform without the sense that *they* are doing it. But when they start to think about what they are doing, they mess everything up. We, as the cold cognitive conscious self, get in our own way. When we get out of our own way, meaning we downregulate our cold cognition, we are in the *zone*.

Reaching dizzying heights with a skill is being able to remain in the zone for longer periods of time. Psychologist Mihaly Csikszentmihalyi referred to this experience as *flow*, which is actually an older Eastern concept. Being in the zone is the heightened level of skill harnessed by world-class performers. Our cold cognitive concentration gives way to a much deeper level of focus. If you are focused, and not thinking, your cold cognition will slowly downregulate and you will be in the zone. The effortless cognitive ease we feel when we are in the zone is when the lights are on but nobody is home, meaning the slow cold thinking function we believe is who we are has shutdown. As a result, the aesthetic beauty of the natural world comes alive through your skill.

Understanding the science of skill demonstrates how human cognition is embodied. So the methods for cultivating a skill should be approached with the new embodied model of the self rather than the hangover of an old and dusty disembodied model. And yet, though the embodied mind may appear new to cognitive science, it is only catching up to an embodied model of mind that is much more ancient. To sufficiently understand how to cultivate a skill and reach peak performance, we need to understand the wisdom and science behind the development of skill as first explored in the East.

2

INTELLIGENT
SPONTANEITY

The embodied model of the self was the primary viewpoint during the Warring States period of China and other parts of Asia. But it is in China especially that we discover the embodied mind model. During the Warring States period there were numerous philosophers and sages whose names we still know today. They were, in historical order, Lao-tzu, Confucius, Mencius, and Chuang-tzu. Though their philosophies may differ somewhat, their way for understanding the mind and body was the same. Their view of human nature was mind-body holism. Their philosophies, social systems, religions, and ritual practices reflect this holistic view. For centuries, ancient Chinese people followed their philosophies and rigorous training to cultivate harmonious dispositions in the self, and they had no doubt that human cognition was embodied. Any other model, such as mind-body dualism, was shown the contempt it deserved.

If the embodied model of the self was understood to be how humans were hardwired, then we can see why a healthy skepticism developed toward mind-body dualism and its rational agents. In the East, in general, the skepticism shown toward rationality has culturally held firm. The battle within us, then, is not between a rational being attempting to lord it over an unruly body but instead is a tug of war between an allocation of function between the two systems of hot and cold cognition.

In the West and the modern developed world, the majority of our energy is allocated to the function of the cold system trying to control the natural hot system. But in the ancient East it was considered absurd to try to overemploy the cold system, since the main driving force and our essential nature were thought to be within the hot system. The focus in ancient China, then, was more about ingrained skill and shaping our character because they can both be cultivated in our hot system as natural and spontaneous.

So Eastern thought, especially the ancient Chinese embodied model of the self, can be seen as (1) an essential corrective to the way modern Western philosophy has a tendency to focus on the cold cognitive aspects of conscious thought, rationality, and willpower and (2) a partial inspiration for the modern revolution of embodied cognition in cognitive science. This is why merging cognitive science and Eastern thought into one coherent model can be helpful for developing skill and attaining peak performance.

Skill Stories of the Effortless Mind in Ancient China

Perhaps no other sage or philosopher during the Warring States period explores the development of skill more than Chuang-tzu. The Chuang-tzu text is like a manual for cultivating skill and training spontaneity, and a lot of other things, which synthesizes well with modern cognitive science. The skill emphasized by Chuang-tzu in his writings is not only about expertise but also life skills, which are supposed to contribute to developing harmonious dispositions in the self. Chuang-tzu, on a subtle level, examines the science of skill and how to reach peak performance to the point of explaining what the actual experience is like.

Chuang-tzu understood that spontaneous skill comes from the deeper, more evolutionary ancient hot system.

Somehow we need to ignite the spontaneity within the hot system naturally. The cold system interferes with the spontaneity of life. Even in ancient China people overly identified with the cold system that gives one this sense of being an isolated self. Chuang-tzu explains that our real nature, the authentic self, is beneath the rational cold cognition. He articulates this through skill stories that exhibit this transfer of functional allocation from the cold system back to the hot system.

Chuang-tzu is one of the most unusual and humorous sages throughout history. His stories of skill reflect his nature. Instead of using examples of musicians, painters, or any world-class performers for his stories, he chose an unusual bunch of misfits, including a butcher, woodcarver, and swimmer and also commended the hunchback and the drunk. Chuang-tzu had a tendency to focus more on the ordinariness of life to showcase the beauty inherent within it. He used the craftsmen as examples to explain how skill and virtues can become so much a part of us (hot cognition) that they are instinctive and spontaneous.

One of the most famous stories in the Chuang-tzu text is about a butcher called Cook Ting (or Butcher Ting). The Cook Ting story setting is a traditional religious ceremony where an ox will be sacrificed in public for the ruler Lord Wen-hui and a large crowd of onlookers. Cook Ting is at center stage for this religious event. This ritual of animal sacrifice demands the difficult skill of using a blade with precise timing and perfect execution. But this appears not so difficult for Cook Ting. He slices and dices the ox up so effortlessly that Lord Wen-hui is astonished. He cannot believe such a mundane skill can reach the heights of beauty similar to an artistic performance. He approaches Cook Ting to ask how he can cut an ox up so effortlessly. Cook Ting explains that after years of cultivating his skill, he now perceives the ox with his spirit, and it spontaneously guides him in the right direction:

What I care about is the Way, which goes beyond skill. When I first began cutting up oxen, all I could see was the ox itself. After three years I no longer saw the whole ox. And now—now I go at it by spirit and don't look with my eyes. Perception and understanding have come to a stop and spirit moves where it wants. I go along with the natural makeup, strike the big hollows, guide the knife through the big openings, and follow things as they are. So I never touch the smallest ligament or tendon, much less a main joint.[1]

Allowing spirit to move where it wants from a contemporary perspective is the spontaneity of the hot system naturally functioning without the hindrance of cold cognitive analysis. When Cook Ting says, "Perception and understanding have come to a stop and spirit moves where it wants," what he is really saying is, "When I have stopped the cold cognitive thinking apparatus, the spontaneous nature of the hot system takes over and moves effortlessly with the environment" (in this case the blade moving effortlessly between bones without touching ligaments or tendons).

And yet this ability of Cook Ting's expert butchery was something that took three years to master. From years of repetition and discipline, the skill of butchery had become as effortless, instinctual, and spontaneous as walking. The need to *think* about what he was doing evaporated. All that was left was a movement of effortlessness that encountered no resistance in mind, body, or environment. Cook Ting and his skill as a butcher were one because the skill was so ingrained in his hot cognition that it was as effortless as walking for him. His embodied mind had reached the height of skill, a state of emotional intuition, or intelligent spontaneity. Intelligent spontaneity is a common experience for the skillful craftsman and is one of the foundational concepts of Eastern thought.

What Is Intelligent Spontaneity?

The main focus of many ancient Chinese sages and philosophers during the Warring States period was the concept *wu-wei*. Wu-wei literally means nondoing, nonforce, and effortless action. The effortlessness of wu-wei is ultimately a state of intelligent spontaneity. However, the concept of how wu-wei is achieved differs slightly among the sages. Chuang-tzu's focus is on skill, which actually adapts perfectly to modern cognitive science.

The effortlessness of wu-wei can be seen in situations where we are trying too hard and not allowing life to naturally happen. For example, when we put a key in a lock and try to turn it too fast, we feel resistance. To unlock the door you need to be loose and relaxed, and when you jiggle the key ever so softly the door unlocks effortlessly. By moving with the lock rather than forcing the key against it you effortlessly unlock the door. The key and door analogy is not only about how expert skill is effortless but also a metaphor for how we move through life.

The story of Cook Ting is about how we can effectively move through the world with skill and not feel resistance. Reaching peak performance is the same: you attain expert skill in your desired craft, and that extends out into life in general. This feeling of effortlessness is a state of psychological ease and emotional intuition we feel through our whole body. The goal of wu-wei, then, is to effectively move smoothly through all aspects of your life, where even unexpected events are dealt with spontaneously and with intelligence. No obstacle is too big or even really perceived as an obstacle anymore. In a state of wu-wei you don't press up against obstacles but instead act in the same fashion as with the gentle key in the lock: when you may absorb the pressure of an obstacle rather than resist it, your actions become skillful and effective. This absorb-and-respond technique is one of the foundational pillars of traditional martial arts.

The foundation of martial arts is wu-wei at its core, cultivating intelligent spontaneity to move perfectly without having to think about it. From the first remnants of spiritually oriented martial arts, with its focus not only on intelligent spontaneity but also health, longevity, and physical immortality attributed to the philosophy of Yang Zhu, until present day martial arts, nothing has fundamentally changed.* But many modern-day martial artists forget that their art is really about intelligent spontaneity, because they are attracted to competition and the chance to appear better than their opponents. This attitude also eliminates one of the primary goals of martial arts, which is to cultivate harmonious dispositions in the self, such as humility, compassion, honor, respect, honesty, and forgiveness.

Transforming your character through martial-arts training is the real proof that you understand the core philosophy of martial arts: there is no opponent other than yourself. Your perceived opponent in martial arts is reflecting back to you what it is you need to change or what it is you need to train harder to overcome within yourself. The idea of a winner and loser is purely a combative approach to martial arts and is in direct opposition to the spiritual core at its foundational roots, which is to cultivate skill to be a better person. And that spiritual core, no matter whether you use martial arts for combat or transformation, is the ability to be in intelligent spontaneity. While modern martial artists (especially mixed martial artists) often use the word *flow* to describe the state of being very lucid and in the zone, this more common understanding of the flow concept is at a novice level and not really at the depth of Csikszentmihalyi's original study.

The spontaneous nature expressed through us in a state of wu-wei is the deeper and more powerful raw material of our hot cognition functioning optimally. It puts emotional intuition into adept action. Without the interference of the overanalytical cold system, you express the spontaneity of human nature intelligently. Intelligent spontaneity, then, is a fully embodied state of mind where one is perfectly calibrated to the environment.

---

*The philosophy of Yang Zhu is known as Yangism. Yang Zhu is credited with "the discovery of the body." There is speculation that the oldest forms of martial arts in China go back to the Xia Dynasty more than four thousand years ago, but there is not much evidence to support this claim and a suspicion that these forms of martial arts were only combat oriented.

The environment essentially becomes an extension of your skill. For example, when you are in a state of intelligent spontaneity in martial arts, you are perfectly calibrated to the obstacles you face with an opponent. The opponent will try everything to land a blow, but you see his movements almost in slow motion. As a result, you act spontaneously without the action feeling like a reaction because there is no conscious thought driving it. And even if you do absorb a blow, you move with it, which is a technique in the Korean martial art hapkido. This makes the opponent overextend and lose balance, usually falling to the ground. In Chinese thought this approach is explained by the concepts yin (feminine/passive) and yang (masculine/active). In Chinese thought, yin nourishes yang. This means that when we are intelligently passive (poise) we give birth to correct action minus aggression. We usually overextend in hapkido (or any martial arts and life in general) when we are full of aggression and emotions. Essentially, if we are not receptive enough we will be hard and rigid. Hard and rigid is easily overcome by someone who is soft and flexible because they have poise and are fully present in the moment. As Bruce Lee once said, "Be like water, my friend."

This effortless cognitive style is similar to the movements of a graceful dancer. Intelligent spontaneity is not only the effect of a dancer's being perfectly calibrated to the environment, but it is the essential goal of martial arts, or any skill for that matter. In a state of intelligent spontaneity we approach life with a mind of no deliberation. An expert craftsman embodies this effortless state of mind. The craftsmen integrate the two systems into mind-body holism, so they are perfectly adapted to the world around them. Though to cultivate expert skill and skill in life we have to understand how a craftsman disengages from the cold system to allow the hot cognitive virtues of nature to spontaneously flower.

The Craftsmen Mind-set

The expert craftsman is a perfect example of how both systems function together to evoke intelligent spontaneity. Their mind absorbed in their craft is a metaphor for how we too can be absorbed fully in life through a chosen skill. A skilled craftsman's integration of mind and body back into its original holism is the result of years of training their embodied cognition to be as natural as nature itself. The craftsman moves effortlessly through their skill, and this is applied to life in general. When the two systems function naturally it is totally normal to be perfectly calibrated to the environment. Edward Slingerland, a professor of Asian studies at the University of British Columbia, explains further:

> For a person in *wu-wei*, the mind is embodied and the body is mindful; the two systems—hot and cold, fast and slow—are completely integrated.[2]

The problem for all of us is how to establish this integration, considering we've gone through extreme social training to be primarily cold system operators. The answer is in the process of the cognitive training a craftsman undergoes to develop their skill. Keep in mind, though, their awareness of the technical language of cognitive science is usually not known. Actually we have all gone through some form of craftsman-like training, but we've had no technical language or modeled framework to understand how to hack into the mind-body integrated system. Well, that is, until now.

To integrate the two systems so that they are working together, we need to develop the ability to concentrate for extended periods of time, which will eventually evoke a deep level of focus that arises from the hot system. Craftsmen can evoke this ability spontaneously anytime if it is needed, to the extent that it is as normal as chewing food. The way the process begins is through the long and arduous training required to call on a skill on command.

The process of learning a skill to this heightened degree is dependent on a strong cold system to begin with. But keep in mind a strong cold system is still dependent on the emotional intuitions of the hot system. For example, many of us will not pick up skills for a particular craft if we have no interest in it. Usually we have to be intuitively attracted to whatever it is, which ultimately gives us the motivation to be better and hopefully reach peak performance. We might gain employment in a job we have no interest in, and yes, we do acquire skills, but it usually stops at gaining the adequate skills needed because there is no intrinsic motivation to excel.

Intrinsic drive cannot be artificially created; it has to be an emotionally intuitive response from the hot system. But without a strong cold system, it is hard to nourish that natural calling to explore your intrinsic drive. So when a craftsman discovers a skill they are eager to learn, hard work has to begin. This means a lot of cognitive load and strain to learn the details must be employed, and nuances must be understood before a skill is embodied (remember the earlier example of my wife's learning to play the violin).

A strong cold system is dedicated to the theory of a particular skill and the discipline required to embody it. We have all tried to get better at something, which requires practice every day. Usually we don't want to use a lot of effort, but something inside says, "Stop being a weakling. Suck it up and push forward." That inside dictator is of course the cold cognition, and it is a strong cold cognition if the message is heeded to push forward.

When a craftsman strengthens their cold system and becomes a dedicated student to whatever skill they're learning, they are ever so slowly downloading the subtle nuances and theoretical details of that skill into their hot cognition. As a result, the skill begins to unconsciously manifest. You can't say why you can now throw the football in a perfect spiral like Tom Brady, but you can surely do it. That ability was once a foreign action, but then seemingly out of nowhere it became second nature.

The hot system can continue to fine-tune a particular skill when a strong cold system has the iron will to reach beyond the known limits. However, as this process continues the craftsman invariably encounters an unexpected snag: the cold system begins to *inhibit* peak performance. Once a skill has become ingrained in the hot system, the cold system is a hindrance because of its tendency to analyze and overthink. When a skill has become embodied the primary way to get better is to continually perform that skill through constant repetition. But this cannot happen if the cold system is still functioning and is essentially in the way. From a contemporary cognitive science perspective, this is what it actually means when we say we are in our own way, meaning the cold system is in the way of the hot system naturally expressing itself.

You, the seat of consciousness in the cold cognition, have to be fired. It is like firing the boss, manager, or coach so that the team can perform without an interfering voice analyzing everything. If the cold system cannot be downregulated, it inhibits intelligent spontaneity. The effortlessness in a performance, no matter what it is, is ruined when we begin to overthink what we are doing. As a result, we regress back into mind-body dualism training. Expert skill and peak performance develop from embodied cognition, mind-body holism.

The problem in attaining skill and reaching peak performance is that we don't know how to temporarily shut down cold cognition. When we are fully engaged in what we are doing, cold cognition is naturally downregulated because parts of the brain are not activated when they are not necessary. And when intelligent spontaneity comes to life, cold cognition is not activated because it is not part of nature's spontaneous beauty. When the spontaneity of the hot system is expressed, through a skill or otherwise, cold cognition is downregulated. But keep in mind that while your cold system is not functioning as it normally does, it has not disappeared. It has simply been reduced to an objective witness scanning the environment just in case something dangerous comes into view.

When skill is ingrained in the hot system, we access, more often than not, that deep level of focus where the sense of "you" doing "something" has evaporated. You have merged as one with the activity. There is no distinction between you and your skill; they are one. As a result you are one with the terrain your skill has to navigate through; i.e., you are in the zone (a deep level of focus in your hot system). The real reason you are in the zone is that your cold cognition has downregulated to let the spontaneous nature of life come alive through you. Essentially, there is no person because the cold system, which is where we identify with ourselves as a person, has downregulated. In the experience of intelligent spontaneity, we come in contact with a deeper level of existence beneath our personality, within our hot system.

This deeper level of existence is where the naturalness of life spontaneously arises. As with martial artists, to cultivate expert skill is a process of coming back to our ancient natural virtuous mind (hot system) through the experience of intelligent spontaneity.

To experience intelligent spontaneity requires discipline, not wishful thinking. But within the hot system we also have natural virtues, such as humility, compassion, forgiveness, and love. We know this because we all feel them, and they feel right. These are natural emotions we don't have to think about because they are spontaneously part of nature. Discipline will evoke and enhance these natural virtues. But when it comes to skill and reaching peak performance, we need to have dedicated discipline and build structure in our life to put the odds of success in our favor.

3

DISCIPLINE AND STRUCTURE

Dedicated discipline and structuring your life requires hard work. Essentially, you need a good work ethic to continually grow your skill. Yet hard work is not necessarily "hard" but rather something you are compelled to keep grinding away at because the sense of growth is satisfying, especially if you are fortunate enough to cultivate a skill that is intrinsically purposeful. Many of us end up in dead-end jobs because either we doubt our own capabilities or we don't have the will to keep going no matter how many obstacles we have to overcome.

To eventually be in a state of intelligent spontaneity, where the cold system has downregulated, requires years of training at a particular skill to make it spontaneously hot. The ancient Chinese sage Confucius said it wasn't until he was seventy years old that the heavenly virtues (hot system training) could spontaneously move through him. In the *Analects,* a text attributed to Confucius, he states:

> At age fifteen, I set my mind upon learning; at thirty, I took my place in society; at forty, I became free of doubts; at fifty, I understood Heaven's Mandate; at sixty, my ear was attuned; and at age

seventy, I could follow my heart's desires without overstepping the bounds of propriety.[1]

Confucius dedicated his whole life to cultivating intelligent spontaneity. His focus was on being an authentic individual with dignity. He had trained his character to the point that he was naturally and spontaneously virtuous. Confucius's teachings, philosophy, and rituals were designed to cultivate wu-wei into our hot system. Though we might be frightened by a lifetime of training, Confucius's steely determination to overcome his warped nature to be natural again is something we can be inspired by. He never gave up, and as a result, the experience of intelligent spontaneity far outweighed the effort that went into cultivating it. Confucius understood that we have a mind-body holistic nature. But he also understood that we are often trained differently, so we cannot just return to our natural state and move skillfully through life without a determination that is unwavering.

Mental Toughness

Many successful people have one thing in common: mental toughness. Similar to Confucius, people who fulfill their potential have an intrinsic drive to be better without being distracted by anything else. What matters most to them is cultivating their particular skill, which in the end brings value to the world. Anything unrelated to their skill is a distraction. Someone who has reached an optimal level of performance has for years developed the habit of eliminating everything that does not support their particular skill. In a world saturated with all sorts of distractions, mental toughness is a strength you need to cultivate.

With the blips, tweets, and so on all vying for your attention, you have to cultivate the habit of remaining focused on your skill, as it will enhance your "grit." Psychologist Angela Duckworth explains the science of grit in her work. She says that it is built on the idea of *Effort × 2*. Effort × 2 is the formula of talent × effort = skill, and skill × effort = achievement. We've all heard of the talented person who never achieved anything. And we've also heard of the super determined but not very talented person who achieved greatness. Reaching our full potential is not dependent on talent, though some does help to begin with. It is our committed effort that takes our talent and skill on to achieve our goals. Wishful thinking will not get you there, whether you're talented or not. You have to put the work in. You must develop grit. Exercising the grit of mental toughness is like giving your brain a workout. Grit is the flexing of the mental muscle. No matter what circumstances come into your life, they do not distract you from your desire to achieve peak performance.

Having grit leads to a healthy obsession for cultivating skill. This is a dedication to go *all the way,* leaving no stone unturned. The idea of going all in is often frightening because it means not only a lifetime of dedication but also that we have to endure failure after failure to evolve on our chosen path. Many of us don't want to face failure because we mistakenly believe failure is an end in itself. But failure is only a stepping stone on the path of growth. You could not achieve anything without failure.

Successful people have endured a multitude of failures. But in the end they recognize that failure is not an inherently negative circumstance. Failure cannot deter a healthy obsession. When you are all in, there is no going back, so be careful what you wish for. Cultivating expert skill requires many failures and even humiliations that should not be viewed as something to run away from but rather as fuel to motivate you to get better.

When we learn to drive a car, for example, we go through many embarrassing situations where we feel humiliated without realizing that driving too will become ingrained in our hot system through repetition. Our "failures" move us forward to become a good driver. Driving a car at first is alien, but the will to be an adult who can look after oneself is the fuel that pushes us through failure. Those who can drive had a healthy obsession to be a driver, and nothing was going to stand in their way.

Your driving skill becomes incrementally better as you continue to drive more often, and eventually the skill becomes ingrained in your hot cognition. The process of developing many other skills is the same, but a lot of expert skills continue to be refined over a lifetime, which is a lot longer than it takes to learn to drive a car.

Developing grit means continually showing up each day to get better. To be perfectly calibrated to the environment through intelligent spontaneity is the result of constant hard work, pure and simple. It is common for people to assume some form of wishful thinking, such as the popular idea of "the law of attraction," will get them where they want to go. But as I explained in chapter 2, Intelligent Spontaneity, fortuitous outcomes are often the result of prolonged training to develop an expert skill and also skill in life. As the famous Latin proverb states, "Fortune favors the brave."

"Dreaming" about succeeding in life is all well and good. But that will do nothing if you don't put into motion what is actually required to achieve those goals. Hard work, not daydreaming about what you want, will get you there. A good example of this is UFC fighter Conor McGregor. McGregor has achieved a lot in the UFC. Early in his career he was attracted to books about the law of attraction, and he somewhat attributes his success to dreaming it into reality. But the truth is that McGregor is obsessed and trains harder than a lot of other fighters. He is 100 percent dedicated to cultivating more skill as a mixed martial artist. All of the years McGregor has been grinding away have evoked an intelligent spontaneity within his skill set. His dreams were lofty and grand, but his grit and obsession are what should inspire you because those are what *truly* got him to where he is in the sport.

Skill, then, is about disciplined action and harnessing intelligent spontaneity. You cannot wish for intelligent spontaneity. Wishful thinking, law of attraction or otherwise, is just the cold cognition speaking to itself (we think people are crazy when they talk to themselves in public, but we say nothing about it when we do it internally, which is almost the same thing). Skill is ingrained in the hot system; no form of magic can implant it there.

You need to be obsessed and gritty to reach your optimal potential. When you are obsessed and gritty you are totally fine with going through a lot of suffering and numerous sacrifices to reach your full potential. You might suffer from years of grinding away at your craft, where progress at times is hard to see (I know this especially as a writer). You could be hanging out with your friends enjoying the sweet fruits of life, but instead you sacrifice your time to a craft that feels bigger than you are to reach your optimal potential, even though sometimes your optimal potential looks like a mirage.

Many of us are accustomed to running away from suffering and do not wish to sacrifice anything to be better. But with mental toughness you can become intimate with sacrifice and suffering to the point where you embrace them. Your willingness to push through a lot of suffering to achieve your goals is a testament to your grit. Instead of being pushed around by life in the process of cultivating skill, you bite down and push forward because you realize obstacles are only temporary hurdles. Actually, the idea of Elysium, of overcoming obstacles to enter a world free from obstacles, doesn't exist. In our life we encounter a never-ending pattern of obstacle after obstacle but are trained by our world to avoid them. If you continually try to avoid obstacles, you will never reach your full potential because it can only be achieved by *overcoming* obstacles.

And yet your optimal potential is not a stationary place you arrive at and remain for the rest of your life. On the contrary, reaching our optimal potential means we're at our best in that present moment in our life. You have pushed the boundaries to be the best version of yourself according to that point in your life, but at the same time you are still evolving. The idea of perfection is an illusion. Your optimal potential is not the obstacle-less state of Elysium, but the ability to continually overcome obstacles and grow as a result. Living a life in accord with the growth mind-set is what perfection really is. So reaching your optimal potential is an ever-growing state of mind, and the only way to harness this growth mind-set potential is to have an attitude and work ethic of steely mental toughness.

Mental toughness is the ability to welcome obstacles, as they hold the key to growth if we have the balls (or ovaries) to face them. Overcoming obstacles requires dedicated discipline and a healthy obsession. It took Confucius seventy years to overcome the idea that obstacles are something in our way. He never reached Elysium, as obstacles persisted. But he did reach a form of Elysium psychologically. The intelligent spontaneity he experienced was a freedom to move through life effortlessly. Obstacles were no longer obstacles. He was perfectly calibrated to the world around him. His skill was like the blade of Cook Ting moving effortlessly through the ox's joints. Confucius is an example of the mental toughness we need to have to be the best version of ourselves. Though we may feel overwhelmed with what it takes to cultivate skill and attain peak performance, Confucius shows us through his life that the freedom of intelligent spontaneity is reached through discipline.

Freedom through Discipline

From infancy to adulthood social training warps our nature (hot system). We are trained along hardened socially accepted lines, which often run counter to our natural intuitions. Social training is centered on enhancing the ability to be primarily rational agents (cold system). As a result, we replace our sense of spontaneity and awe with an analytical view of the world where we slice and dice it up to try to make sense of what the hell this life is about. Instead of enjoying the beautiful dance of life, we would rather sit back and make calculations about it, as if it can be measured.

Trying to remain analytical and rational has warped our naturalness and made the world stale and joyless, which are some of the hallmarks of a "no room for error" secular world. Without nourishing the spontaneity of the hot system, we can feel no real deep-down joy in the world, which leads to the rational opinions that contribute to conflict, debate, arguments, and ultimately unnecessary war. Our innate child-like innocence is rubbed out in favor of the illusion that we can come to a logical conclusion on all matters (even a logical meaning for life, which is absurd).

Earlier I mentioned the childlike innocence that still exists in some parts of rural India. This innocence really does humble our so-called all-knowing intelligence because we intuitively sense this innocence as an innate natural aspect of our mind. In the affluent developed world, we have lost this innocence. As a result we have a common tendency to think we know what is best for the rest of the world.

Chuang-tzu was suspicious of anyone who thought they knew what was best for the rest of us. He didn't believe there was one right philosophy or way to behave and act in this world, and he was a skeptic of those who tried to teach a certain philosophy. This is why he was sometimes critical of the Warring States period sages and philosophers such as Confucius and Mozi. Chuang-tzu's focus was on how to cultivate intelligent spontaneity, so we can move skillfully through life without regressing into the lowly motives that drive society.

As we discover in Chuang-tzu's skill stories, we need to foster methods to disengage from cold cognition to allow the natural hot system to flourish—though allowing naturalness to flourish is paradoxical. We cannot just *be* naturally spontaneous because our nature is warped from social training. What we actually need is to *train* ourselves to be natural.

Disciplined training evokes our innate naturalness. Dedicating our discipline toward this goal will restore our original hot cognitive nature minus the cold cognitive social ticks that were implanted in there over the course of our life. This paradox of disciplining yourself to be your natural self again is something extensively studied and explained by Eastern thought, especially Zen Buddhism. Physicist Fritjof Capra explains the Zen approach to this paradox through the difficult naturalness of the Zen master Po-chang:

The perfection of Zen is thus to live one's everyday life naturally and spontaneously. When Po-chang was asked to define Zen, he said, "When hungry eat, when tired sleep." Although this sounds simple and obvious, like so much in Zen, it is in fact quite a difficult task. To regain the naturalness of our original nature requires long training and constitutes a great spiritual achievement.[2]

Po-chang's simpleness of mind evokes intelligent spontaneity. He didn't have to think about what he should do or be because there was no artificial split of mind-body dualism in him. He was as free as Confucius was at seventy, where the spontaneous virtues of mind are expressed authentically. Po-chang was not a victim of overusing the cold system. Though his naturalness may appear difficult to our culturally developed minds, it is not something to be frightened of but instead embraced. Zen embraces this paradox, and the mind of Po-chang is the inspiration to move forward with discipline. As I mentioned earlier, Confucius's dedication to discipline is proof that the freedom of intelligent spontaneity comes naturally after years of training.

Zen master Shunryu Suzuki elaborates on this idea of experiencing freedom through discipline. After Suzuki arrived in the United States from Japan he started teaching Zen to Americans. He would explain to his students that we have this innate spontaneity in harmony with all life, but we need to discipline ourselves to experience it. As a result, Suzuki's students would often ask him why we should worry about all the hours of meditation if, deep down, we are already natural. Suzuki would reply by stating that though it is true we are all buddhas, the reason we meditate is that that's just what buddhas do. It is through discipline, in this case meditation, where we experience the mind free of cold cognitive overload. Discipline *itself* is what evokes a free person, or one who is perfectly calibrated with the environment and world through intelligent spontaneity.

It doesn't matter whether it is through years of meditation, writing, or training as a musician or an athlete, discipline evokes effortlessness:

our ability to be in the zone. From a cognitive science perspective, discipline downregulates cold cognition. This allows the ingrained discipline in the hot system to function intelligently in connection with spontaneity. Essentially, you hone your skill and reach peak performance when "you" have disappeared. The wisdom of the body (hot system) knows exactly what to do after years of discipline.

As I mentioned earlier, the premise of martial arts is to reach intelligent spontaneity, and that can only occur through constant training. The same is true in Zen, where extensive training is also undertaken to experience intelligent spontaneity, or to *be* in Zen to use Zen Buddhist terminology. Zen has interesting methods and techniques to achieve this. One is called a koan. *Koan* is a Japanese word referring to a riddle passed down from master to student.

Zen masters use koans to test their students' progress in Zen, meaning how spontaneously the student answers the riddle. The master essentially wants to see the student react spontaneously, without *thinking* about the answer. Here's an example of a koan: A master and his two students sit before a pitcher. The master says, "Without calling it a pitcher, tell me what it is." One student replies, "It cannot be called a piece of wood." The master is not at all pleased with this overly clever verbal response. The other student, however, simply knocks the pitcher over and walks away as if nothing happened. The master is extremely pleased by his actions because his response demonstrates a deep understanding of Zen.

Though this koan method may appear like utter buffoonery, and the masters themselves as mere buffoons, it is really genius for cultivating intelligent spontaneity. The koan is designed to train you sufficiently enough to be able to give an immediate emotionally intuitive answer. This trains the student to act with intelligent spontaneity, without thinking, a mind of no deliberation. After years of meditation and daily mindfulness, the mind becomes more than capable of tackling a koan no matter how absurd it may sound. Koans train you to act without the cold system interfering with natural spontaneity. This has been referred to as the "oomph" of conscious will and effort because that is what it feels like when our cold system continually interferes with nature's hot processes. Koans are a remedy for this cold cognitive habit.

The amazing effect koans have on our ability to be intelligently spontaneous is immense. The intention of Zen koans is to encourage people to naturally be their authentic self, to display mind-body holism. So at the beginning of koan training there is no real, correct answer for irrational riddles. But this trains you to be fully present and ready to act spontaneously without any need for prompting. As a result, when you leave the Zen monastery you are now equipped with the skill of intelligent spontaneity.

The end result of koan training, then, is that not only do you respond to life spontaneously, but you also attain a skill for giving the perfect intuitive solution to a problem. You will not only act with immediacy, but your actions will also be appropriate to whatever situation presents itself. The so-called buffoonery that koans promote actually trains you to be more authentically yourself without identifying with the cold system. This is also one of the end goals of Confucian training. Think of Confucius at seventy, and you have an accurate description of someone who responds in perfect accord to what the world conjures up.

As you can probably guess, being able to act spontaneously and be correct is extremely difficult, so having discipline and a dedication to cultivating intelligent spontaneity is not something we can whimsically approach. Discipline needs structure. To be trained in koans, meditation, mindfulness, and Zen, we need a monastery with order and structure to best facilitate our discipline. Likewise with any skill we wish to develop, environment matters.

Rig the Game to Win

Structure helps maintain discipline so that intelligent spontaneity can flourish. In a Buddhist monastery, for example, every little thing is deliberately designed to facilitate deep states of meditation more often.

Those people who have spent extensive time in a monastery can usually go deeper in their meditation than someone in society who practices twenty minutes every morning. In the monastery environment you harness the skill to go into a deep calm in your meditation, which you then bring back to your normal life to practice daily.

The difference between those who dedicate the time and effort to learn and practice meditation in a monastery and those who learn meditation from books, YouTube, meditation groups, and so on is the setting and structure of the monastery itself. This is not only true for the skill of meditation; it is true for almost all skills. Whatever your skill may be, you should immerse yourself in an environment that helps it grow. For example, if you want to be successful in business you ought to first find a good company and businesspeople to learn from. When we are constantly immersed in an environment conducive to our desired skill, our cold system slowly learns all the technical ins and outs, and as a result, they all become ingrained in our hot system, whether we like it or not.

The more you engross yourself in a conducive environment the more you will absorb all of the subtle nuances and expert skills unconsciously. If you want to be a great chef, first find a great kitchen with a master chef. Then, once you have learned all you can from that teacher, it is time to become the master yourself. Being in service to a master of any skill tends to speed up the process for reaching peak performance. Having a mentor in business, for example, is a well-trodden path to success. In all walks of life, in any skill, this student-teacher relationship helps you not only develop skills but also witness emotional intuition in action. Learning from another's expertise and successes teaches you to be truly humble and not egocentric.

Strategist and writer Ryan Holiday calls this the *canvas strategy*. The canvas strategy is a great practice for inculcating humility and reducing your ego. By following the canvas strategy you essentially have to become a great student in complete service to your mentor. To do this you need to live by principles that include handing over great ideas to your boss/teacher/mentor/master, producing more than your fellow students or colleagues and giving those ideas away to them so that everyone can benefit, and taking on the work that nobody wants.

These methods of the canvas strategy, and many others, help strengthen discipline in structured environments, which facilitates successful outcomes. Holiday himself is a good example of the canvas strategy. Instead of following the conventional path to success, he dropped out of college at nineteen to apprentice under famous author Robert Greene, whose books such as *The 48 Laws of Power* and *Mastery* have been extremely influential. Apprenticing under Greene is what set Holiday's life in a positive direction. By following the canvas strategy Holiday went on to become the director of marketing for American Apparel at 21. He eventually started his own company, Brass Check, which has advised clients such as Google, TASER, and Complex and also many best-selling authors. Holiday has also written six books. He achieved all of this at a young age by earnestly following the canvas strategy. His apprenticeship gave him structure and discipline, which became the building blocks for future success. The conditions for success were set for Holiday under Greene.

Structured environments allow us to nourish our particular skill, which in the end gives us the best possible chance to succeed. If you set the conditions in your favor, then you can rig the game to win. Rigging the outcome really depends on the structure you build and follow, which nurtures your discipline and ultimately enhances your skill. If you don't have a discipline with structure, then rigging the outcome becomes much more difficult.

A good example, again, is UFC fighter Conor McGregor. In 2016 McGregor was slated to fight Rafael dos Anjos for the lightweight championship of the world. This would be McGregor's chance to gain a second championship belt to match his featherweight championship at the time. But less than two weeks out from the fight, dos Anjos broke his foot and could not compete. McGregor still wanted to compete, so a fight with Nate Diaz was organized at welterweight for no championship.

McGregor was on an unbeaten run in the UFC, and many experts and fans were tipping him to win. But Diaz had other plans. McGregor dominated most of the first round, landing many blows to Diaz's head. But in the second round everything changed. McGregor was noticeably getting tired, and Diaz began to land headshots that were stunning McGregor. In a panicked daze McGregor shot for a desperate and lazy takedown, which you definitely don't do when you are fighting a Brazilian jujitsu black belt. As a result, the fight went to the floor, and Diaz eventually landed in top position and began to ground and pound McGregor. McGregor turned on his stomach, which gave Diaz access to his back. This is like bread and butter for a black belt like Diaz. As a result, Diaz got a rear naked choke on McGregor and got him to submit in easy fashion.

After the fight it was evident that McGregor had legitimate holes in his game. His cardio was terrible and his jujitsu skill left much to be desired. McGregor didn't shy away from these facts, and he set a course to rectify them. He wanted a rematch with Diaz, and it was granted by the UFC. But he recognized his training methods had to change or the result would not. Before his first fight with Diaz, he had no structured training regime. So he spent a whopping $300,000 on his training camp in Las Vegas to prepare for the rematch. His whole life became structured to facilitate discipline and cultivate skill. He had structured training times, a guide on what and when to eat, free time, a sleep schedule, and so on. This is not uncommon for professional athletes, but it was something McGregor had to embrace because he realized he could not just rely on his talents and rest on his laurels. He brought in Brazilian jujitsu black belt Dillon Danis to coach him, and he also worked extensively on his cardio.

All of these little adjustments helped McGregor to cultivate more expert skill as a mixed martial artist. He followed this routine for the entire training camp in preparation for the Diaz rematch, and in the end, all of the hard work paid off: he won a close fight by majority decision. McGregor had rigged the outcome so he could win, literally.

The better we become at rigging the outcome with structure and discipline, the easier it is to build momentum. Having structure develops more discipline, which in turn drives an unstoppable momentum that propels us forward to achieve our goals one after the other. Building momentum is a by-product of repetition, of doing something over and over again. The more we continue to rig the outcome through structure and discipline, the more momentum will be guiding us to the front of the pack.

The Melbourne Storm, a rugby league team in the NRL, has been a perennial title contender year in and year out for over ten years. They were the first team in Australia to recognize that to have consistent momentum, they needed structure and discipline. As a result, they have had an astonishing winning percentage of 69 percent* since 2003 under coach Craig Bellamy, who is widely regarded as the greatest coach of all time. Much of the Melbourne Storm's success can be attributed to Bellamy's radical ways of thinking and genius.

Bellamy was the first coach in the NRL to recognize that goals can only be achieved consistently through a set structure and disciplined work ethic. He applied a systematic approach to lifestyle, training, and how to win games. It was a foreign concept to other teams. After a game Melbourne players were heard in interviews explaining how their great win and performance could all be put down to following their systems and processes. Ten years earlier nobody would have known what the players meant by such a statement.

Everybody in the NRL wants to achieve the goal of being the Premiers (competition champions), but the idea of following a system was thought of, at the time, as just a lot of nonsense. People plainly assumed that Melbourne was simply a far better team than the rest. But the remarkable thing is that even when Melbourne lost great players because of salary cap constraints, they would sign free agents or discards from other teams and turn them into legitimate superstars by applying the mysterious systems that the team followed.

---

*This percentage stat is from 2003 to the end of the 2019 season.

The Melbourne Storm were sporting-world pioneers in the idea of valuing system focus over goal orientation, and there is actual scientific logic to this method. Following systems is different from striving for goals. Adam Alter, associate professor of marketing and psychology at New York University's Stern School of Business, explains in his work that being goal oriented keeps you in a failure state until you reach your goal. This means that as you evaluate your process all you get is the negative feedback of having not achieved that goal (until you get close to the goal; then there might be some positive feedback). On the other hand, following a system allows you to incrementally build momentum, where you begin to experience achievement in your life more regularly. Following a system becomes a goal over and above the goal itself.

In fact, following a system is psychologically healthier than being goal oriented. The reason is that goals are broken processes. When we reach a goal we invariably feel empty. As a result, we anxiously chase the next goal we set ourselves because our goal didn't nourish us psychologically. If we perceive goals as a sort of signpost, they feel like a massive anticlimax once we reach them.

Developing skill, especially reaching intelligent spontaneity, has nothing to do with goal setting. Intelligent spontaneity is evoked by a system of structure and discipline we trust and follow to the nth degree. A dedication to a systematic approach for your skill must overshadow your desire for attaining goals if you want to truly succeed (I explain this further through four fundamentals to create a masterpiece day in the next chapter, chapter 4).

If you trust a system you will achieve your goals continually because structure and discipline help momentum become an unstoppable force in your life. The Melbourne Storm trust their system no matter what happens. Even when they are losing a match with time running out they don't panic; they trust the system to get them out of the dilemma. And invariably it does. Their dedication to hard work and structure, not to mention the individual selfless attitude for the good of the team, puts them out in front of the pack. It's an environment where an average player can turn their career around, ironically not by being a better player but instead by just playing their small role in the systems the team follows. As with any sport or profession, those who excel are the hardest workers with sufficient structure in their life.

To reach peak performance requires you to remember that while you're relaxing, someone else out there is obsessed about the same skill and accruing a lot of momentum you don't have. To level the playing field and put the odds of success in your favor, you need to have the same healthy obsession. Showing up each day consistently will fuel momentum, and you will surely excel.

People often attain expert skill and succeed in life not because they are better than we are but because they are the ones who showed up every day willing to work and grind. We can't just dream big and think it's going to happen. We can't just focus on the obvious stuff in our skill training and think we are going to reach peak performance. As Conor McGregor and the Melbourne Storm realized, *everything* matters.

The Little Things Matter

Unless you focus on the fine details, your skill will not go too far. Everything matters, even the seemingly unrelated things. This is still not a widely accepted view. When we examine expert skill we need to realize that simple things like having a healthy diet and good sleep contribute to better results. What we do away from our skill training is usually thought to be irrelevant. If you believe this, you will not succeed or reach the greatness of those who know how relevant everything is. The littlest things contribute to greatness.

In sports they often speak about taking care of the 1 percenters. Actually, in some cases athletes mainly focus on the 1 percent plays because that is the foundation of everything else. The 1 percent plays are the fundamentals of any craft that we often forget as we develop more skills. Many people who reach greatness actually don't get too far ahead of themselves because they practice the fundamentals consistently. They become highly skilled at the fundamentals. This allows them to extend their skill incrementally with patience. Those who try to cut corners are often exposed in time. They end up being the "coulda, shoulda, woulda, but *didn't*" cases.

After you read this book, there will be no reason for you to end up in the coulda, shoulda, woulda category. I want you to go *all the way*. Leave no stone unturned, nourish the fundamentals to reach greatness. The 1 percenters are crucial if you want to reach your optimal potential.

To cultivate expert skill and reach peak performance you have to have structure and discipline centered on the fundamentals in your lifestyle. The lifestyle we have, though seemingly unrelated, is what contributes to success. Our lifestyle fundamentals are what give us the greatest chance at being at our optimal potential. In part 2 you will learn what it takes to follow the optimal fundamentals to train like a champion.

PART 2

Training

4

THE FOUR FUNDAMENTALS

Our lifestyle habits determine our performance. Every little thing we do in our life matters. It is not enough to train hard at a particular skill and then go home and veg out in front of the television. We need to have discipline in our ordinary lives as well. If we focus on the 1 percenters (fundamentals) in our lives, everything else will be nourished. We benefit from keeping our lives simple, so we should focus on the simple things. Nourishing the 1 percenters and keeping it simple has to be our mind-set if we seek to reach our optimal potential.

If you want to cultivate skill and reach peak performance, you need to train like a champion. You need to acquire the habits and routines of world-class performers. Those habits and routines may appear unrelated to your skill, but they hold the key to your reaching your full potential. An athlete, for example, who indulges too much in unhealthy food and alcohol will most likely never reach their optimal potential, even if they're talented. Something as simple as what you eat affects your overall performance. We often neglect the simple things that make us human; those simple things we cannot do without.

Our basic needs such as eating healthy food and getting adequate rest are often neglected. Our lives have become so busy that we develop eating habits that are unconscious and reduce our sleeping hours to pack more work into the day. This attitude is disastrous. It damages the human mind, contributing to mental health issues, including panic attacks, chronic anxiety and stress, depression, and schizophrenia, to name just a few. We obviously want to avoid such mental health issues if we wish to have an optimal life. In many modern people this excessive busyness and stress are so ramped up that our fight-or-flight response is stuck in the *on* position. This ever so subtly depletes our energy reserves, leading to fatigue and mental health problems. As a result, we seek stress management solutions that are in reality still promoting a stressful life-style because our core habits are not being addressed. I'm not interested in the typical stress management like many health practices. Instead, I want to explain to you a peak-performance lifestyle structure that keeps stress from developing because you are managing your well-being rather than managing your stress. As spiritual teacher Sadhguru explains:

> Stress is not a part of your life. Stress is just your inability to manage your own system. Stress happens not because of the nature of your work. The Prime Minister is complaining of stress, the peon is also complaining of stress. In between, every other person is saying his job is stressful. And those who are unemployed also find their situation stressful. So you are suffering your job—if I get you fired, will you be joyful?
>
> No. So stress is obviously not about your job, isn't [is] it? It is just that you do not know how to manage your body, your mind, your emotions, your energy, your chemistry—you do not know how to manage anything. You are functioning by accident, so everything is stressful. If you get into a car where if you turn the steering wheel one way, the car goes in the opposite direction, you'll be stressed, isn't it [won't you]?
>
> Right now, that's the kind of mechanism you are driving. Without understanding anything about it, just by chance, you are blundering

through life—so you will be stressful [*sic*]. Stress is not because of the nature of the activity that you are performing or because of life situations. Stress is simply because you do not know how to manage your own system.[1]

Having a structure in our life is essential if we wish to accomplish our goals. To be at your optimal state you need to follow the four fundamentals of life that have been tried and tested by many successful people before you. These fundamentals are meditation, nutrition, exercise, and adequate sleep. They are the paint we use to create masterpiece days, and each day should be approached the same way a true artist approaches a blank canvas—with a readiness to tune in to emotional intuition. Developing expert skill and reaching peak performance depends on these four fundamentals. They are the structure and the little 1 percenters that build success if we continue to practice them daily.

Though these four fundamentals may appear simple enough, many people find them hard to follow because their minds are so accustomed to seeking distraction. This happens because we don't really know the ins and outs about how to practice these fundamentals properly or to employ the methods and techniques that are essential to helping us achieve masterpiece days. In the following sections I will give you the know-how to create a peak-performance lifestyle by allowing these four fundamentals to become a deeply ingrained part of your daily life.

Meditation

Meditation is fairly common nowadays. People want to be able to focus better, and meditation is the best practice to harness that ability and the peaceful state of mind that was the original purpose behind meditation. Meditation methods can range from the absurd to the profound, but if we can separate the wheat from the chaff we can discover pure gold.

Posture

When I mention meditation, I am referring to its traditional context: sitting cross-legged with an upright spine. This is nothing against meditative techniques such as hatha yoga, t'ai chi, or any other movement method. They can be sufficient methods but are actually extensions of the traditional practice. So methods such as hatha yoga and t'ai chi can be practiced, but they should be done secondary to traditional meditation. We should adhere to the traditional meditation posture as much as possible. Having the spine erect is primary. As for your legs, if you are not capable of a full lotus posture (see figure 4.1 on page 78), try a half lotus posture (see figure 4.2 on page 78). If neither of these postures is comfortable, try the Japanese style of sitting on the balls of your feet (see figure 4.3 on page 79). This posture can be assisted by placing a thin cushion between your buttocks and lower legs. If you cannot do any of these, just sit cross-legged (see figure 4.4 on page 79). Or if all else fails, just sit on a chair.

A comfortable posture is important for a lengthy meditation habit, but you may feel the slightest tension after a while, no matter which posture you choose. Please don't fall into the habit of trying to avoid tension by changing posture all the time. A little bit of tension will assist your ability to remain mindful during meditation practice. But don't go crazy and let the tension become so painful that it ruins your meditation practice. Just a little bit of tension is enough to remain alert to the subtle sensations within the physical body.

Ritual*

Making meditation a daily ritual is essential. You want to be extremely particular when it comes to meditation. You don't want to practice it haphazardly like sitting down to surf the internet or read a book.

---

*This section on ritual is for religious and nonreligious people alike, as is the case with everything else in this book. Sacred images and objects are tools for meditation and useful for developing an atmosphere. They are *not* meant to convert you to any religion or belief. Such things can be viewed for their aesthetic value rather than their cultural significance. Keep this in mind if you are apprehensive about consecrating your home or concerned about what people will say.

Figure 4.1. Full lotus posture.
Illustration by Dao Stew.

Figure 4.2. Half lotus posture.
Illustration by Dao Stew.

Figure 4.3. Japanese style posture.
Illustration by Dao Stew.

Figure 4.4. Cross-legged posture.
Illustration by Dao Stew.

Instead you want to ritualize it. Atmosphere matters; it sets the stage for deep levels of meditation. Atmosphere is why monasteries, temples, and ashrams are more often than not built in nature, away from all the noise and the monkey mind of society. When people visit such places they usually go to a level of quiet in their mind that they have not previously experienced.

I've taken people to Bodh Gaya in India, the place where the historical Buddha became enlightened under the famous bodhi tree. Built in front of the bodhi tree is the Mahabodhi Temple, where Buddhists and non-Buddhists from all around the world visit. The atmosphere here can be quite overwhelming. Some of the people I've taken there have been moved to tears by the sheer heartfelt feeling of the people within the place, all dedicated to compassion for all beings. On top of this, the same people report being able to attain a deep level of meditation, which I can attest to as well. It is the atmosphere that facilitates such deep levels. And even though it is amazing to visit places such as Bodh Gaya, you can bring the same level of quiet to your home. But you will need to build an atmosphere to replicate the experience.

Consecrating your home is essential for a peaceful atmosphere. I'm not promoting idolatry, but it can be beneficial to have some sacred object in your meditation area. Maybe a sculpture of the Buddha, a Shiva Nataraja, or an image of a symbol such as the Om or the yin-yang might do. It really depends on your taste. Around such sacred objects it is good to have some candles set into decorative candleholders to enhance the mood. Incense adds a delicate touch to building atmosphere. It stimulates the suppressed sense of smell and brings an aromatic tranquility to our meditation room or space.

The use of incense is quite specific. First of all, the type of incense you buy is important. There is a lot of incense out there that is mass-produced and made very cheaply. Those types of incense can be toxic and are best to avoid (be sure to read the contents label before burning the incense). My favorite incense is made in Auroville, India, by a company called Mystique. It is made of all organic elements and has an aroma that instantly puts your mind in a peaceful place. Second, we need to know what to do with incense. I learned from Buddhists and Hindus how to use incense as a practice.

In the morning before meditation you should cleanse your home with incense. This means that you slowly walk around your home spreading the incense smoke everywhere, especially around sacred objects or things you value. While you do this you recite a mantra, either verbally or in your mind. I recite Om Namah Shivaya not only because I personally love this mantra because of its meaning and ancient significance,* but also because it is easier to say than a lot of other mantras. This incense cleansing practice with a mantra allows you to practice gratitude for the life you were given and the life you are creating and also develops an atmosphere in your home that best facilitates the actual practice of meditation.

Practice

There are so many methods of meditation that it is hard to know where to start. A lot of meditation techniques out there are just fancy and weird for the sake of being different. A lot have no practical or psychological effects. The most tried-and-tested techniques are the ones that have the most profound effect, and they are usually the simplest to follow. So don't be worried; I'm not going to play mystical kung fu with your mind using a bunch of woo-woo nonsense. I am going to share with you the most effective methods and techniques of meditation. But first, what is the core objective of meditation? The answer is equanimity. Meditation is supposed to help you slowly develop an equanimous mind. The following methods and techniques are not only for quieting the mind but also for inner transformation.

---

*Om Namah Shivaya means "adoration to Shiva as the one absolute universal consciousness of everything" or "universal consciousness is one" or simply "adoration to Lord Shiva." Shiva in this context is a representation of the ultimate reality of the universe known in Sanskrit as Brahman.

One of the most beneficial meditation methods in the world is *vipassana*. *Vipassana* is a Pali word that means "insight into your true nature," and it is thought to be the original teaching of the Buddha. Vipassana meditation teacher S. N. Goenka made vipassana popular through a ten-day course for practicing its technique. Those ten days are composed of ten hours of vipassana meditation a day (one hundred in total for the ten days) and two light vegetarian meals before midday. Males and females are segregated, and eye contact, physical contact, and talking with other people are not permitted. This throws us completely inward, where we become super conscious of our interior landscape. Hence, insight into your true nature.

The vipassana meditation technique is a science for getting down to the sensory level of our psychosomatic organism. The sensory level is believed to be where we transform our subconscious because its impulses are at the root of the mind-body matrix, and the impulses at the root level are those unconscious sensations. The purpose of the vipassana meditation technique is to transform our subconscious to be free of the conditioning that clouds our perception of the world and leads to suffering. To achieve this, we need a good anchor for meditation. *Anchor* is a word commonly used in meditation that refers to a place where we put our awareness in the process of meditation.

The anchor in vipassana meditation is the breath. In vipassana this is known in Pali as *anapanasati*, which means "awareness of respiration." Breathing is an activity that is unconscious most of the time. Just ask yourself this question: Did I remember to breathe today? It's an odd question. The majority of us would answer no because it is something that unconsciously goes on and on without the need of our awareness. But in vipassana those ordinary unconscious activities of the body are what we place our awareness on.

In the vipassana technique of anapanasati, we are taught to place our awareness on our breathing without altering its natural rhythm. The problem is that when you begin to think about what you're doing, you will change its rhythm. It does take time to master this skill, but when you do it is super effective for bringing equanimity to your mind. The end result of sufficient practice of anapanasati is that you will become super conscious of the subtle sensations in your body and the subtle thoughts in your mind because you've transferred your awareness from breathing to the sensory level.

The science of vipassana, transforming yourself at the subconscious level, is possible if you practice this advanced technique daily. Those of you who cannot spend extensive time in a monastery can practice this technique for thirty minutes first thing every morning, and if you want to reap the ultimate benefits, practice thirty minutes before bed as well.

Other techniques of meditation focus on the breath as well. In Zen Buddhism there are numerous techniques. I will mention only three here, two of which are centered on breathing.

The first breathing technique is focused on inhaling deeply and exhaling every last bit of air. On the inhale you want to breathe down into your lower abdomen. You actually want to see your belly button region moving out. When we are stressed or busy, our breathing is very shallow and only our chest expands. But with this practice you are pushing air into the lower part of your lungs that are usually deprived of oxygen. When your lungs are full and your lower abdomen has expanded, hold the breath for five seconds and then exhale slowly to the point that there is no air left in your lungs, then you hold that breathless state for five seconds and then inhale deeply again. If you continue to repeat this process earnestly your mind will become extremely quiet, to the point that the process of this meditation has dropped away because your mind has completely settled without the sense of "you" doing anything.

The second breathing meditation technique in Zen is similar to vipassana, except the anchor is counting. In this technique we place our awareness on our natural breathing, and we start counting from one with the first inhale, two on the exhale, three on the next inhale, and so on. As you continue this process, if your mind starts to wander in thoughts, then you have to go back to one and start over. If you are fortunate enough to get to fifty without thinking, then you should be entering a deep state of meditation. And if somehow you get to one hundred, then the counting process will most likely have dropped away as your mind has come back to its original tranquility. This will most likely happen before one hundred, but I'll give that number to you as a general marker.

The third Zen meditation technique, known as "open-awareness meditation," is different from the previous two breathing meditation techniques and is more commonly used. Open-awareness meditation is focused on becoming conscious of mental activity. We place our awareness on the stream of consciousness, which is all the thoughts that continuously bubble up in our mind, including all the stories we tell ourselves. Zen master Thich Nhat Hanh says that when we are unconscious of the stream of consciousness, we are like cows ruminating on food, but the food human beings are ruminating on is thought.

In open-awareness meditation it is interesting to discover that when we observe our thoughts, they disappear like ghosts. The more we practice open-awareness meditation, the more we put into jeopardy the validity of some of the thoughts we have rattling around inside our skull. As a result of consistent discipline, our inner landscape begins to become more tranquil, the waves of thoughts begin to cease movement, and our mind becomes as transparent and reflective as an undisturbed lake.

Another meditation technique used across various traditions in Asia involves the tongue. I call this method the "sleeping tongue meditation." Obviously this meditation is focused on the tongue. What many people don't know about the tongue is that when there is tension within us, the tongue is usually stiff, pressed against the palate and behind the front upper teeth. We are usually not conscious of this fact. An amazing way to release this subtle tension is to rest the tongue in the lower jaw, almost like it is floating. As soon as you do this you will be far more relaxed and the feeling of tension will decrease. The difficulty with this meditation is keeping the tongue in that relaxed state. Once our attention is drawn to thoughts you will notice the tongue has become stiff and pressed against the palate and front upper teeth again. But if you can keep the tongue relaxed, this meditation is very effective.

Once you are off the meditation cushion, it is time to bear the fruit of your practice in ordinary life. The purpose of many meditation methods is to make us more mindful in our everyday activities. Your meditation practice will make you more conscious in conversations and daily tasks. You will be able to focus more deeply in your creative life, and you will have a greater ability to be completely present, without excessive thoughts and internal chatter.

Once you have adhered to the posture, rituals, and practices of meditation, it is important to understand its long-term effects and the scientific explanation behind them. Let me explain.

Science

The science of meditation is best understood through cognitive science (revisit chapter 1, The Embodied Mind, to refresh your memory). In the act of practicing meditation we are attempting to downregulate the cold system within the PFC. In the meditative process you are essentially eliminating yourself, leaving behind just a deep level of presence. That presence is the natural witnessing state of the hot system. It is objective rather than subjective, as subjectivity is a function of discernment within the cold system.

The more we downregulate cold cognition through meditation, the more we access pure presence. We ultimately harness a deep level of focus that allows us to be super absorbed in whatever it is we are doing. Our mind's habit for seeking distractions diminishes. Actually, research on people practicing meditation, especially mindfulness, reveals a decrease in activity in the lateral PFC, which suggests that a flexible openness in the hot system circumvents the conscious mind. What is important when we are focused (in the zone) is the activity at hand, which could be writing a book, playing a sport, gardening, listening deeply in conversation, and so on. You are completely present without the psychic pull of the past and future distracting you.

Consistent daily meditation will transform your mind back to its original embodied cognition. It becomes easier to be authentic and spontaneous without falling back into overrationality and the error of hot intuition. We begin to exude a meditative state of consciousness in our ordinary life off the meditation cushion. This effect is not only because we are continually downregulating the cold system but also because in the downregulation process we are stimulating the parasympathetic nervous system (PSNS). The PSNS, which is one branch of the autonomic nervous system, is activated when we are in a relaxed state. It is responsible for "rest and digest" and "feed and breed" functions that occur when the body is at rest, especially after eating, including sexual arousal, lacrimation (tears), salivation, urination, digestion, and defecation. Regularly stimulating the PSNS through activities such as meditation allows us to maintain this system as our baseline rather than the hyperalert, "fight or flight," stress-based sympathetic nervous system so many of us live in on a daily basis. As a result, we are extremely calm because we do not need to be actively engaged in every little thing. Being externally inactive and internally inactive (not reacting to thoughts and emotions) facilitates this calm state, which transforms our behavior.

The long-term effects of meditation are evident in our behavioral patterns. Instead of being thrown here and there by the world, we become more aware of how our mind reacts to the world on a subtle level. In three of the major Hindu philosophies—Vedanta, Samkhya, and classical yoga—they explain this meditative transformation through two key Sanskrit terms: *viveka* (discernment) and *vairagya* (nonreaction). Harnessing the ability to remain a witness to your mind's activity for extended periods is viveka. This capability in turn strengthens your ability to not react emotionally, which is vairagya. Discernment and nonreactiveness change our behavioral patterns, and they are both a by-product of consistent meditation.

The benefits of these long-term effects are immeasurable. In our social life we begin to speak less, listen more, and react less. There are always social situations with other people such as friends, family, and colleagues that will press our buttons. Most people are accustomed to reacting emotionally without having the discernment to catch such frustrated emotions. A daily meditation discipline enhances the ability to not react, allowing certain situations to be as they will be without any need for emotional input. You will actually become perfectly fine not reacting to negative situations, even if it is something directed at you personally. Your usual offended reaction will lose its pull in your mind, as things of a larger magnitude take central focus.

Meditation gives us the clarity to observe our minds and not over-react to a world always vying for our attention. It is essential for skill and peak performance and a fundamental for optimal living. It also enhances our ability to focus deeply to evoke intelligent spontaneity. On top of this we become more pleasant people to be around. A meditative state of being contributes to all facets of our lives and the decisions we make.

Nutrition

What we should and shouldn't eat is becoming increasingly confusing in an age swamped with information. There are numerous fad diets out there, and many are attached to health gurus. Some have no scientific basis and are tinged with pseudo information. I'm not going to join the growing roster of health gurus and introduce my own fad diet. The role of this section is to explain how following a healthy diet is one of the fundamentals for optimization, though I will mention some practical health tips based on modern science and ancient Eastern health systems. But before we get into *what* we should eat, let's talk about *how* we should eat.

Mindful Eating
Eating, like breathing, is often an unconscious activity, especially in the modern world, where people are in the bad habit of eating while

watching something on the television, smartphone, tablet, or computer. As a result, eating becomes secondary to the entertainment we are consuming. This habit is terrible for the mind, as it enhances anxiety and stress—we are naturally analog and not digital, meaning we function better doing one task at a time and are not designed for multitasking even though we can do it.

Mindless eating leads to an erratic mind and bad health because our watching-screens-while-eating habit is usually based on the illusion that we don't have enough time, which causes anxiety, and our meals are centered on foods that are quick and easy to make, such as processed food and fast food, which are not the best choices for optimal health. Mindless eating is a bad habit of the excessively busy, which, unbelievably, many people aspire to become.

Mindful eating, on the other hand, is a healthy habit that will uproot our impetus toward busyness and multitasking. The practice of mindful eating is essentially about slowing down to focus on chewing and swallowing each bite. The way you practice is to put the food in your mouth and chew it thoroughly into a lather before swallowing. We usually don't chew our food enough because we are always in a hurry and anxious about what we are going to do next.

Another core component of practicing mindful eating is that we should thoroughly chew and swallow one bite of food before we load up our spoon, fork, chopsticks, or hands with another. We are accustomed to putting food in our mouth and immediately loading up the next bite and getting ready to shovel it in, even though we haven't finished chewing and swallowing the first one. Slowing the eating process cultivates patience. You train yourself to wait until you have finished one spoonful before loading up another. The use of chopsticks can also be beneficial for mindful eating and cultivating patience. I've been using them for nearly ten years, even for such food as salad. They have definitely been a great tool for concentrating on my eating.

The whole process of mindful eating transforms your angst into gratitude and appreciation for the food you have. Instead of eating being a laborious task we do secondary to other more "important" matters, it becomes the central focus.

Mindful eating is also about teaching that the things we commonly assume are ordinary—such as eating—are actually extraordinary. It is the so-called extraordinary matters—such as busyness and entertainment—that are truly secondary to our ordinary humanness. Don't believe me? Then refrain from watching anything and eating anything for as long as you can. Which urge requires your immediate attention first? We all know the answer to that.

Another key factor in mindful eating is moderation. Our organs usually have to work double-time to digest and process the amount of food we pile on our plate. The modern buffet seems like a good idea, but it has disastrous consequences. If our stomach is bombarded with too much food, our mind becomes agitated because our organs are linked to our brain, and if they are having trouble absorbing all that food, then your well-being will be affected. All we truly need is three simple meals a day with no snacking in between. In a lot of ashrams and monasteries they will take this one step further by just having breakfast and lunch. Some Buddhist monks and laymen, such as those who stay at the late, great influential Buddhist teacher Ajahn Chah's Wat Nong Pah Pong main monastery and Wat Pah Nanachat international monastery, both in the Ubon Ratchathani province of Thailand, will only have breakfast. This type of extreme moderation keeps the mind settled so the monks can enter deep states of meditation.

Another method to practice to enhance moderation is intermittent fasting, which I practice quite often. Intermittent fasting entails having your first meal at 12:00 p.m. and your next meal before 6:00 p.m. This is only two meals a day within a six-hour window and a total of eighteen hours a day without any food. This method of fasting, along with others such as a three-day water fast, repairs the body and helps it come back into balance. With all of these moderate approaches to eating, our digestive system begins to function normally without the habit of passing excessive amounts of food through the system. A moderate diet will help you to be more creative, conscious, and alert in your day and to reach your optimal potential.

Disciplined Eating

Our modern eating habits are not totally defined by a lack of awareness or wrong dietary choices. Instead they are often the result of a lazy cold system allowing the more ancient hot system to run wild as it seeks excessive fats and sugars that once upon a time were hard to obtain. Edward Slingerland explains the constant challenge the cold system has in trying to override the evolutionary needs of the hot system:

> So if I say that I had to force myself not to reach for that second helping of tiramisu, there is a more than metaphorical struggle going on. My conscious, cold system, which is concerned about long-range issues like health and weight gain, is fighting to control the more instinctive hot system, which really likes tiramisu and doesn't share my cold system's concerns about the consequences. This isn't because hot cognition doesn't take future consequences into account. The problem is that this system's conception of relevant consequences was fixed a long time ago, evolutionarily speaking, and is fairly rigid. "Sugar and fat: *good*" was for most of our evolutionary history a great principle to live by, since acquiring adequate nutrition was a constant challenge. For those of us fortunate enough to live in the industrialized world, however, sugar and fat are so widely and freely available that they no longer represent unqualified goods—on the contrary, allowing ourselves to indulge in them to excess has a variety of negative consequences. The great advantage of cold cognition is that it is capable of changing its priorities in light of new information.[2]

I will discuss components in our diet, such as sugar and fat, shortly. With a disciplined diet you are not giving your mind the chance to succumb to cravings for pizza, a can of Coke, ice cream, and so on. If you set up a disciplined diet, then you give your mind a template for eating that actually promotes good health. A disciplined diet contributes highly to health and well-being because most disciplined diets are focused on whole foods and not processed foods. A disciplined diet trains you not to reach for the next sweet, for example. And a disciplined diet transforms our lazy dietary habits.

Personally I've experimented with a lot of diets. I was a vegetarian and part-time vegan for six years. I felt great for a long time. But I then began to feel that I was lacking animal proteins and healthy fats. So I switched to a low-carb Paleo diet but periodically change to a ketogenic diet when I feel the need (I'll explain this diet shortly). I've followed this diet for four years, and I feel healthier than ever. But this diet might just be right for me. I'm not concerned about what diet you follow because I believe all diets have their pros and cons.

What *is* important is discipline. It is important to be conscious of what you put in your mouth. Many people don't even consider the food they eat and just assume the socially accepted food pyramid is the way to go, even though diseases such as cancer and diabetes are on the rise. Eating is a base need we often neglect. Studying foods and diets is therapeutic because it means that you are beginning to take your power back.

According to Eastern health systems, such as Ayurveda, our psychosomatic organisms are constitutionally different. So when you are studying it is best to find a diet that suits you at that particular point in time. Your diet may change over time through further study and experimentation, but it is healthy training for the mind to be disciplined in what you eat so the mind doesn't veer off into distracting tendencies such as yearning for junk food.

Disciplining our diet is the first part of the battle to reclaim our health, which is fundamental for reaching our optimal potential. So it doesn't matter whether you are on a Paleo, ketogenic, primal, vegan, or vegetarian diet. What matters is your dedication to a diet through discipline. Something as fundamental as eating must become conscious if we are to reap the rewards of optimal health. But even though discipline is essential, there are certain foods that are healthy and others we should avoid that stretch across all diets.

Food Choices

There are certain rules to follow with our diets. Discipline is great, but we also need some rules that are not negotiable for our health and well-being. For instance, the accepted notion that fat is bad and carbs are great has to be reevaluated, and thankfully it has been in modern science. Sure, there are certain fats, such as trans fat, that are not the best, but healthy fat in general is not what makes us overweight and unhealthy; excessive carbohydrates do. People gorge themselves on loaves of bread and bowls of rice and wonder why their waistline is expanding. "I don't eat fried food like French fries," they say, and that is great, but then you see them eat a foot-long sandwich as if all that wheat is supposed to be good for them. Well, it isn't. That flabbiness and those puffy skin rolls so common in the modern body shape are the result of an excessive carb-centered diet.

We all know the culprit of an unattractive beer belly, but we don't want to look at the elephant in the room with regard to obesity; namely, grains—especially wheat. Our habit of eating excessive wheat, rice, and grains in general is terrible for us. For example, wheat, especially the refined variety, enhances our chances of disease and obesity and affects brain health. If you want an optimal state of mind, then excessive grains should be avoided. One of the main reasons is gluten. Gluten is a mixture of proteins found in wheat and other related grains. It is something we should avoid at all costs if we want a healthy brain and tranquil mind. But if you go gluten free, you must eat a small amount of dietary fiber from gluten-free fiber-containing grains once a day, or ideally, just a couple of times weekly, such as amaranth, buckwheat, millet, quinoa, rice (brown, white, wild), sorghum, and teff (yes, I said rice, but remember all of these grains should be consumed in moderation). But fiber doesn't have to come just from grain.

It can also be found in foods rich in prebiotic fiber such as jicama, onion, garlic, chicory root, dandelion root, and Jerusalem artichoke, to name just a few.

Neurologist Dr. David Perlmutter explains the health issues concerning gluten and the brain:

> Gluten is a foreign protein to human physiology, and is the cornerstone of leaky brain—causing inflammation. Science has made some amazing discoveries about the blood-brain barrier in recent years, most importantly that it can become just as permeable as our gut lining. When gluten is introduced to the body, it turns out that it is inflammation that degrades this important barrier.[3]

Consumption of refined flour and an excessive amount of grains is what we must avoid no matter what diet we follow. Instead of eating a salad sandwich, just eat a salad; it won't kill you. We need to avoid habitually eating any type of fillers, which are usually carbs such as bread, rice, and potatoes. Eating these carbs excessively is detrimental to your health. Along with fillers we should avoid refined sugar (sugar is a carbohydrate, after all). Sugar is in a lot of our foods and drinks, anywhere from pasta sauce to baby food and milk. The sugar in a lot of processed foods and drinks is usually fructose, which occurs in inert sugar, honey, and a great many fruits. But this is not to beat up on fruit; fruit is healthy for you in moderation. But if you are consuming a few mangoes and some dried fruit a day, for example, then that is far too much sugar intake. Fruits such as blueberries and avocados are low in sugar and full of nutrition.

We are unknowingly addicted to sugar. Every day on average people exceed their daily sugar consumption. Someone will have a burger meal and wash it down with Coca-Cola and think it was great until that low depressive feeling from too much sugar comes along (sugar is found in fast-food burgers and basically any poor-quality food). Excessive sugar will mess with your mind and overstimulate your nervous system. Both excessive grains and sugar lead to numerous psychological problems and nervous system diseases. Depression and epilepsy are often managed or cured by simply changing our diet to a low-carb lifestyle. Gluten and excessive sugar consumption are both instrumental in the development of Alzheimer's disease. Dr. Perlmutter explains sugar's connection to Alzheimer's and two simple lifestyle choices to reduce the risk of this disease:

> While our government invests millions of dollars in finding a pharmaceutical to prevent Alzheimer's, study after study has continued to find evidence that through slight variations in our daily diet as well as dedication to exercise, we can have a marked effect on reducing our risk for Alzheimer's as well as actually improve brain performance. Studies have come out linking increased blood sugar with a reduction in the size of the hippocampus, the brain's memory center. What does this mean? It means we shouldn't be surprised to learn that predicted growth in the number of Americans with Type 2 Diabetes is coupled with similar growth in the number of Americans expected to be diagnosed with Alzheimer's in the coming decades.[4]

Another habit we can kick to the curb is eating processed food. Nowadays we are bombarded by processed food in the supermarket aisles. It's popular because it is quick and easy and packaged nicely, which reflects our "get it now" culture, built on the illusion that we have no time. In fact, many people throw up the no-time-to-prepare-a-meal excuse to justify their bad eating habits. We all have time; some more than others, but nevertheless we all still have it. The real problem is that we fill up the spare time we do have with frivolous entertainment, which ultimately keeps us in a stupefied state. Essentially, we become so lazy that we lose awareness of our own self-care.

Fall back in love with creating healthy meals with whole foods, preferably organic. Your psychosomatic organism will give you a high five, meaning you will feel great. Eating *real* food will give you everything you need to function optimally.

Next on our hit list for an optimal diet is caffeine, especially the amount that is distributed through coffee, certain teas, and many energy drinks. Our coffee culture is addicted to a feeling that is borderline obsessive-compulsive disorder (OCD). The speed and intensity with which caffeine hits our mind is evident in the speech and actions of those high on it. With the growing trend of cafés on every corner, many people are becoming addicted. For someone who doesn't drink coffee, I find it increasingly difficult to converse with people high on caffeine because their mind is so agitated that they resemble a fidgety kid with attention deficit hyperactivity disorder (ADHD).

Coffee depletes our nervous system, which in turn contributes to anxiety and psychological problems such as panic attacks and depression. A lot of people believe coffee helps them focus. But though you may be sharp and alert, you have no real clarity because the mind is going off like lights on a Christmas tree. Excessive caffeine agitates our mind and compels us to act. We often burn out or feel low after coming off a caffeine high. The problem is that many people just refuel when they are lacking energy and then continue to push their limits without realizing they are draining their energy systems while causing long-term damage.

Sleep is another aspect of our life that caffeine disrupts. Every waking minute a chemical called adenosine is building up in our brain, increasing our desire to sleep. This is known as sleep pressure. Adenosine is artificially muted or masked when we ingest caffeine. Nevertheless, adenosine continues to build up. Once your liver filters caffeine from your system, all of the adenosine that has been silently building up comes flooding back into your system like a dam that has burst through its walls. This phenomenon is commonly known as a "caffeine crash." But you may argue that you drink your coffee (or your last coffee) in the late morning or early afternoon, so it doesn't affect you at night. It is true that levels of caffeine circulating in our body peak thirty minutes after drinking. But the problem is that caffeine is very persistent, which many people don't realize. In pharmacology, they use the term *half-life* for a drug's efficacy. Half-life simply refers to the length of time it takes for the body to remove 50 percent of a drug's concentration. The average half-life of caffeine is five to seven hours. So, sneaking in an afternoon coffee has the potential to disrupt your sleep many hours later.

For these reasons and many more, coffee is considered to have little, if any, value as a food in traditional Chinese medicine (TCM). The science in TCM explains that coffee produces too much yang (heat) in the body, causing the body to be out of balance with yin (cold). Too much heat—or in this case, too much coffee—leads to being too active and thinking too much. Chinese medical doctor Brendan Kelly explains the effects of coffee:

> For many of us, drinking coffee can produce a long list of symptoms . . . and can contribute to, or create, a wide range of [others], including anxiety, racing thoughts, insomnia, disturbed dreams, headaches (including migraines), acid reflux, irritable bowel syndrome, a wide range of stomach and intestinal issues, fibroids of all kinds (including uterine fibroids), growths of all kinds (including tumors), a wide range of skin conditions including eczema, arthritis, a wide range of pain conditions (including fibromyalgia), heart palpitations, excess anger and aggression, dizziness and vertigo, lower-back and leg weakness and pain, a lack of rooted energy in general. In fact, all chronic and acute conditions that involve heat from the Chinese perspective and inflammation from the Western perspective are likely exacerbated by coffee.[5]

A healthy alternative to coffee is tea. There are numerous teas available that have a calming effect, even though some of them, such as green tea, have a small quantity of caffeine. Green tea, oolong tea, and pu'er tea are just some healthy alternatives. Personally I consume master herbalist Ron Teeguarden's Spring Dragon Longevity Tea every morning after breakfast. It contains no caffeine. Teeguarden believes this is the number one tea in the world for many reasons. It has many beneficial herbs, but none more so than the longevity herb *Gynostemma,* or jiaogulan. Jiaogulan is an adaptability-enhancing antiaging herb. In China, health conscious people have been consuming jiaogulan for thousands of years, and in general people live a long and prosperous life. Jiaogulan is known by the Chinese people as "magical grass." Spring Dragon Longevity Tea takes premium grade jiaogulan leaves and infuses them with five premier tonic herbs: luo han guo, *Schizandra, Lycium, Astragalus,* and eleuthero (also known as Siberian ginseng). The bonus with Spring Dragon Longevity Tea is that it keeps you sharp and alert without the drug-like buzz coffee gives you. This whole book was fueled by Spring Dragon Longevity Tea.

Another healthy tea option is masala chai, a famous Indian tea (masala chai literally means mixed-spice tea). Masala chai uses black tea and the spice mixture of ground ginger and green cardamom pods as its base and includes other spices such as cinnamon, cloves, fennel seeds, nutmeg, peppercorn, and star anise. Masala chai is the most popular beverage in India, where you'll find many people during the day stopping off at a tea shop for a quick cup.

There is something mysterious about the masala chai mix that stimulates deeper thoughts and promotes our creative, emotional intuitions. Masala chai is my go-to tea for getting people to think deeply. My wife and I often get into some deep conversations drinking masala chai at our favorite tea shop on the famous Girivalam Road in Tiruvannamalai, India (this is where many worldly renouncers, or sadhus, live). We call these sessions tea *satsangs* (a Sanskrit word meaning "to sit in the company of a wise teacher discussing deep philosophical thoughts and wisdom"), which is the nature of Japanese tea ceremonies in Zen Buddhism.

One thing to be mindful of with masala chai is the amount of black tea it contains. In India it is popular to have a strong Assam black tea. This type of black tea can be too strong, full of caffeine. If there is too much caffeine, it can have an effect similar to coffee. My wife often makes her own masala chai mix without black tea. Finding a company with the actual handmade mix with low black tea content is far better than the multitude of chai tea bag options available on the market (a lot which are not really masala chai). Try to stick to the natural handmade masala chai mix.

Supplements

Eating healthy, nonprocessed foods should provide all the nutrients you need to function optimally. However, if you are still eating a mostly processed diet or feel you are not getting enough nutrition from your healthy diet, there are certain supplements you might want to consider. One is magnesium. Because processed foods diminish our magnesium levels, taking a magnesium supplement will help to stabilize your levels, which will actually get rid of a lot of latent anxiety. Magnesium is also one of the best antiaging minerals.

Another supplement to consider is docosahexaenoic acid (DHA). It is derived from fish oil or algae, and it is also in human breast milk. A DHA deficiency has been linked to many disorders, including dementia and chronic anxiety, so it is considered a necessary supplement for neurological health, which explains why breastfeeding is so important for a baby's neurological development. There are a lot of fish oils on the market, and they are usually combined with eicosapentaenoic acid (EPA), which is completely fine. I've tried a variety of them, and most have been great. Whichever type you choose, you want to make sure that your DHA daily intake is 1,000 mg for optimal benefits.

B vitamins are very beneficial for nervous system support (vegans can be low in B vitamins, especially B12, so it's important for them to source plant-based foods that have B12). There are numerous brands on the market for you to consider.

Another supplement I use personally for my joints is glucosamine. I'm an ex-rugby league footballer, and at the age of twenty-two I tore my anterior cruciate ligament (ACL). At that point in my life I was almost broke, so I lived with that injury until I was thirty, when I received knee reconstruction surgery. As a result, glucosamine is necessary for the health of my joints, and it might be something for you to consider, especially if you are a physical performer (or ex-physical performer like me).

Last but not least are supplements that support the adrenal glands. The adrenal glands are two small glands located on top of the kidneys. These glands produce a variety of hormones we cannot live without, including adrenaline and the steroids aldosterone and cortisol. Cortisol is what helps us respond to stress. It is released by the adrenal glands in response to fear or stress as part of our natural fight-or-flight mechanism. With the constant bombardment of stimuli leading naturally to stress, we are producing high levels of cortisol. Elevated cortisol levels increase our risk for depression, mental illness, and lower life expectancy (on top of a host of other health issues such as lower immune function and bone density, weight gain, heart disease, interference with learning and memory, and the list goes on and on).

The alternative-health community believes that such symptoms lead to *adrenal fatigue*. The scientific community is divided on this topic, as there is no scientific evidence to support it, so it is not recognized as a real diagnosis by the medical community. I'm not going to throw my hat into the ring and argue for one over the other, even though I don't believe that science gives enough credit to alternative medicine, especially traditional Chinese medicine (TCM) and Indian Ayurveda, both of which have been practiced for thousands of years. But what I will say is that elevated cortisol levels are a real problem, so anything to support the adrenal glands should be considered as part of our daily diet.

Adaptogens (adaptogenic herbs) have been imperative in the fight against stress for thousands of years. They can normalize bodily imbalances and support adrenal function, and as a result, they counteract the adverse effects of stress. Adding adaptogens to your diet can make you more resilient against the damaging effects of high cortisol levels. Some of the main adaptogens to counteract stress are ashwagandha, Asian ginseng, holy basil, *Astragalus* root, licorice root, *Rhodiola* root

(*Rhodiola rosea*), and *Cordyceps* mushrooms (though they are not considered an adaptogen in the classic sense). In TCM there are tonics and supplements laden with adaptogens that are supposed to nourish and restore our *jing*,* which supports adrenal and kidney function. While many of these adaptogens can be helpful, don't go crazy and start taking all of them, as this might be too much for your body to handle. There are plenty of adrenal and cortisol support supplements available with a good mix of adaptogens. Do your homework when it comes to the multitude of supplements on the market.

Eat Like a Champion

NBA star LeBron James is a perfect example of how something as simple as a disciplined diet contributes to peak performance. Even though James was already one of the best basketball players in the world, he did not rest on his laurels. A true champion's mind-set recognizes that there is always room for improvement. James already had enough skill, but he wanted to be at his optimal potential more often, basically seeking to have intelligent spontaneity on tap. He recognized he had some weight issues that needed to be addressed.

To become a champion means you understand that the little things do matter; diet is no exception to the rule. Many of the greatest champions in sports follow a strict diet, and James came to recognize the importance of diet. As a result he embraced a low-carb lifestyle. In a little over two months he lost a lot of weight by eating only whole foods, with a reduction in carb intake and strictly no processed foods. This transformed his life and ingrained long-term healthy dietary habits.

This fundamental change in his lifestyle led to great success. His motivation was to help his team, the Cleveland Cavaliers, bring an NBA

---

*Jing is a notion that makes up part of the Three Treasures in TCM alongside *qi* (vital energy) and *shen* (spirit). It is stored in the kidneys and defines our basic constitution. It is our essence, or genetic stock, and it determines the power and vitality of our life. Jing is naturally depleted in our life, and death is determined by loss of jing. TCM believes that the use of adaptogens replenishes and restores our Jing leading to longevity.

championship back to his home state of Ohio. The city of Cleveland was thought to have a "sports curse" because its last championship of any major league sport was in 1964 when the Cleveland Browns won the NFL Championship Game (this was two years prior to the first Super Bowl). James, Ohio born and bred, yearned to end this curse, and eventually all his hard work paid off. In 2016 the Cleveland Cavaliers won the NBA Finals, and James was named the NBA Finals MVP. James and his teammates ended the dreaded fifty-two-year Cleveland sports curse. That small change in lifestyle, which we don't often believe is related to success, had a significant impact on his performance, which in turn had a positive impact on his teammates and the state of Ohio.

Disciplining his diet with a low-carb lifestyle lead to a greater ability to focus and be in the zone. And there is actually science that suggests that the diet itself contributes to greater alertness and concentration. James's diet was borderline ketogenic, which may be one reason for his greater ability to focus and be in the zone.

A ketogenic diet consists of a macronutrient ratio of 60 to 75 percent of calories from fat, 15 to 30 percent of calories from protein, and 5 to 10 percent of calories from carbs. The exact amount of fat and protein needed depends on individual body responses and how active we are. The low-carb, high-fat ratio of a ketogenic diet mimics fasting physiology. It eliminates excessive carb intake and curbs our sugar addiction. When our diet is centered on excessive carbs and sugar, then we are constantly living on blood sugar (glucose) as our primary energy source, which is disastrous, especially to our brain. When we start to transition from carbs to healthy fats as our primary source of nutrition, our liver begins to convert fatty acids to *ketones*, and our body and brain begin to use ketones derived from stored or ingested fat.

Research indicates that ketones are our optimal brain fuel. When we start burning ketones instead of glucose we enter a metabolic state known as *ketosis*. When you are in a state of ketosis your mental alertness and ability to focus deeply are at an optimal level. Forget about coffee; it has nothing on ketosis. In a state of ketosis it feels as though we are in the zone more often than not. I follow a low-carb lifestyle, and sometimes I intentionally design my diet to increase my healthy fat consumption to be in ketosis, especially if I'm writing a book. Some of the effects I feel from being in ketosis are identical to the research: increased energy, alertness, and ability to concentrate; fewer sugar cravings; reduced anxiety; and a good mood that is hard to fluster. Becoming fat adapted is essential to the process of transitioning over to ketones as your source of fuel and is what reduces sugar cravings. Ketones are a longer burning source of fuel than glucose, which needs a top up regularly, leading to all sorts of health issues. In other words, sugar creates a limited amount of energy, while fat creates a lot of very clean energy that lasts for a long time.

Training your body to burn fat first for energy is the key to losing weight just like LeBron James. According to Dr. Cate Shanahan, a scientist and nutritionist who worked with NBA player Dwight Howard and is the science consultant for the Los Angeles Lakers, it's all about training our body to burn fat for energy instead of carbs. This is what it specifically means to be *fat adapted*. Shanahan is not really focused on her clients being in ketosis but rather for them to be fat adapted.

If you are fat adapted on a ketogenic diet or other low-carb diet, you are satisfied for longer periods of time, naturally leading to weight loss and well-being. Actually, the ketogenic diet is considered by experts as the best diet for weight loss. It is also used to treat epilepsy and cancer. Actually the diet was originally developed to treat epileptic children. But keep in mind, a ketogenic diet is not a long-term option for everybody. Dr. Dominic D'Agostino, an associate professor in the Department of Molecular Pharmacology and Physiology at the University of South Florida Morsani College of Medicine and a senior research scientist at the Institute for Human and Machine Cognition, explains why the ketogenic diet doesn't work for some people:

> If your triglycerides are elevated, that means your body is just not
> adapting to the ketogenic diet. Some people's triglycerides are ele-

vated even when their calories are restricted. That's a sign that the ketogenic diet is not for you. . . . It's not a one-size-fits-all diet.[6]

Former ultraendurance athlete and physician Dr. Peter Attia also explains:

Keto works well for many people, but it's not ideal for all. It's also not clear why some people do well for long periods of time, while others seem to derive max benefit from cycling. If certain markers get elevated (e.g., C-reactive protein, uric acid, homocysteine, and LDL particle numbers), it's likely that the diet is not working properly for that person and requires tweaking or removal.[7]

The fact that this diet doesn't work for everyone shouldn't be an excuse to continue gorging on carbs and sugars. It is good to experiment and find your balance according to your constitution. Even though I find the benefits of being on a ketogenic diet great, I still regularly eat fresh fruit in moderation. Disciplining your diet allows you to listen to your body more carefully, so when my body is crying out for an apple, I don't start playing an intellectual game with nature's requirements. But you need to be able to discern between a "need" and a "craving." Otherwise you'll be kidding yourself into believing you need a certain food when you really don't need.

There is a diet designed to address our carb cravings. The slow-carb diet was made popular by serial entrepreneur Tim Ferriss. The slow-carb diet incorporates some of the cravings we have for certain foods and carbs without trying to exclude them altogether. Usually when we try to eliminate certain things our attraction to them is intensified. So the slow-carb diet says rather than being in conflict with yourself, indulge a little instead. For example, on the slow-carb diet carbs such as beans and legumes are acceptable in moderation. Your plate should be split into thirds: beans/legumes, protein, and vegetables. But you should still avoid white starchy carbohydrates such as bread, pasta, potatoes, rice, and sugar including fruit (avocados and tomatoes are fine). This diet, like most healthy diets, is focused on whole foods. The added advantage of a slow-carb diet is that you have one day a week to go nuts, but not over the top. Tim Ferriss aims for Saturday as his day to indulge.

Many people on a ketogenic diet also incorporate this idea, and it is commonly known as "carb day" or "cheat day." On this day you won't want to eat fast food or anything like that. But through the week you want to make a list of yummy food you can make at home that breaks up your dietary routine. For example, I might crave a salami and salad sandwich on rye with mustard sauce, plus a chocolate milkshake made with grass-fed milk. If I'm in the mood to go out I will go to my favorite breakfast restaurant for a Mexican breakfast, and then for lunch I will go to my favorite Indian restaurant. Usually throughout the week I will make a mental note of the food I feel like eating and then on my special day (usually a Saturday) I enjoy the sweet fruits of life. This one day a week gives you one day a week to feel human and helps keep you from developing bad daily dietary habits. If you are not an extremist, then the slow-carb diet is for you. But if you are extreme and follow a strict ketogenic diet, then one day off a week to live a little might be the best medicine.

Experiment for yourself, but please don't become a fundamentalist. Too often people will find something they resonate with and become a "Bible thumper" about it. There is no one fundamental diet for all, only certain food choices and rules we should follow because they are natural. Forget about fundamentalism and ongoing useless debates between vegans and meat eaters, for example. Just eat as naturally as you can and use a disciplined diet to ingrain healthy habits if necessary. Eating as natural as possible is the foundational bedrock for health and well-being.

Retired NRL star Cooper Cronk is a meticulous and highly disciplined individual. He is one of those people who stays as far away from processed food as possible. He basically eats only food that grows out of the ground and livestock. As a result, his mental acuity and attention to detail is second to none. Eating naturally gave him the structure and discipline to excel, finishing his career with a remarkable four NRL Premierships from nine NRL Grand Finals, which is unheard of in the modern era.

A natural lifestyle is essential in nourishing the fundamental of nutrition. A healthy diet leads to healthy habits and more energy for life and benefits exercise, the next fundamental on tap for discussion.

Exercise

In a world that is addicted to sitting, movement is secondary. Actually, the amount of time we sit each day is a relatively new habit. We are naturally adapted to move and are supposed to move a lot throughout each day, but our modern lives—including many of our jobs—are more geared toward sitting. For example, I am sitting while I write this book.

Our general mood and well-being depend on how much we move throughout the day. Our ancestors moved quite a lot more than we do, and they didn't have half the physical and psychological problems we have. Many people who suffer from diseases such as depression, obesity, chronic anxiety, and so on often don't move a lot.

Moving around turns on certain chemicals in our brain that help nourish an optimal state (I will discuss this shortly). Those of us who aren't fortunate enough to be able to walk a lot during the day need to implement exercise routines we can stick to. Along with daily meditation and proper nutrition, exercise is another fundamental for a masterpiece day and peak-performance lifestyle. Even if you do walk a lot, intense exercise will help you immeasurably. Exercise, as with the other two fundamentals, sets the day in a positive direction and makes the likelihood of its being a highly productive day very high. However, exercise itself has to become an ingrained habit. Building structure and discipline for exercise is essential.

Daily Routine

When you exercise is important and does, of course, depend on your daily commitments. Some people have time in the morning to exercise, and some have time at night. Some world-class performers prefer to exercise at night, choosing very late night routines because of their busy schedule. If your day can only be shaped to a nightly exercise schedule that's fine. But if you exercise too close to bedtime it will be difficult to drop your core body temperature to invite sleep. At least two to three hours before bedtime is best for a night workout.

There are significant advantages for exercising in the morning, especially early, just after waking up. Tom Rath, an author and consultant on employee engagement, strengths, and well-being, explains the long-lasting effects of morning exercise:

> When a team of researchers assigned a group of college students to exercise, then tracked their mood the next day, they made a surprising discovery. After just 20 minutes of a moderate-intensity workout, the students were in a much better mood compared with a control group of students who did not exercise. The researchers expected this result based on previous findings. What surprised them was the *durability* of this increase in mood. Students in the group who exercised continued to feel better throughout the day. They were in a better mood 2, 4, 8, and even 12 hours later.
>
> *A mere 20 minutes of moderate activity could significantly improve your mood for the next 12 hours.* So, while working out in the evening is better than no activity at all, you essentially sleep through and miss most of the boost in your mood.[8]

So an early morning exercise routine puts your day in a positive motion where your creativity and life are more vibrant and alive. Hollywood actor and professional wrestler Dwayne "The Rock" Johnson starts his daily exercise routine super early, at 4:00 a.m. Johnson is one of the most charismatic and productive people in Hollywood. His positive attitude toward his work and life in general can somewhat be attributed to his disciplined exercise routine. But not all of us can wake up at 4:00 a.m. every day, and you don't have to. If you can consistently exercise between 6:00 a.m. and 9:00 a.m. four times a week, then that is more than enough. That three-hour window is the best for maximum benefits. But any other time is still good for your health, though you are not reaping the rewards of the twelve-hour benefits.

What you do in your daily exercise routine is as important as when you do it. Walking, for instance, is something we should naturally be doing a lot of each day. Our world is so busy that we need to schedule time for walking because typically most of us wake up in the morning and only walk to our car and then walk to the office, where we sit for the majority of the day. We are definitely in a bad situation if we don't walk at least 7,000 steps a day. The UK National Obesity Forum recommends 7,000 to 10,000 steps each day to stay moderately active. Japan's Ministry of Health, Labour, and Welfare recommends 8,000 to 10,000 daily steps. But we should strive for at least 10,000 steps a day for optimal health. Our body is designed for frequent movement, and 10,000 steps is our basic requirement for sustaining optimal health. As scientist and author Katy Bowman says, "Walking is a superfood. It's the defining movement of a human."[9]

Ten thousand steps is roughly five miles or nine kilometers. The time it takes to walk five miles is somewhere in the ballpark of one hundred minutes, which is not that much time, actually, considering the amount of hours we have in a day. Keep in mind that these 10,000 steps don't have to come from a single hundred-minute walk. They can be accumulated throughout your day by using the stairs instead of the elevator, going for a brisk ten-minute walk on your lunch break, taking a stroll after dinner, and so on. But the average person doesn't get anywhere near these markers. According to the UK's National Health Service, the typical British person walks on average 3,000 to 4,000 steps each day. A similar study showed Americans to average around 5,000 steps, the Japanese around 7,000 steps, and the Swiss and Western Australians around 9,000 steps.[10] As a result, we have tried to turn something that is our natural movement into a scheduled exercise routine. This is why people go to the gym and walk on a treadmill.*

While walking 7,000 to 10,000 steps is necessary to be healthy, we need to include high intensity workouts in our exercise routine to reach peak performance. Just twenty minutes of aerobic exercise a day is enough for optimal health and well-being. But those twenty minutes should be intense. Instead of going for a brisk stroll for twenty minutes, try intense running or bike riding. And the twenty-minute marker can just be the beginning. With increased fitness you can slowly push up to forty minutes or an hour if you feel like superman. Push your limits to be fitter and healthier. I usually ride a bike for forty minutes, which is about twelve and half miles (roughly twenty kilometers), twice a week on top of strength training. If I have time, depending on how busy my week is, I will squeeze in a running session for thirty-five minutes, which is about three and a quarter miles (roughly six kilometers). Sometimes I alternate between running more in a week than riding and vice versa. While I know that my levels are nowhere near the amount of exercise a professional athlete undertakes, they are perfect markers for me to function optimally.

If you're just starting out, you want to begin at the twenty-minute marker and work your way up. Strength training is also important for strength and muscle development. It can consist of lifting weights, gymnastics strength training, or using your own body weight through practices such as hatha yoga. Dr. Peter Attia explains the health benefits of strength training:

> There is value in exercise, though, and I think that the most important type of exercise, especially in terms of bang for your buck, is going to be really high-intensity, heavy strength training. Strength

---

*Unless you have no other option, please don't use the treadmill for walking. It is far better to walk more in your ordinary life, preferably in nature, and leave the treadmill for running.

training aids everything from glucose disposal and metabolic health to mitochondrial density and orthopedic stability. That last one might not mean much when you're a 30-something young buck, but when you're in your 70s, that's the difference between a broken hip and a walk in the park.[11]

Having a few strength sessions a week is imperative. And it doesn't necessarily need to be heavy lifting; you can use light weights for a good muscle burn. It really depends on what fits you best. But keep in mind strength training should be an extension of your cardiovascular training. If you can incorporate aerobic exercise and strength training into your weekly routine, then you have a significant advantage for reaching your optimal potential in whatever it is you do. And if you are fortunate enough to have more time than most, learning Eastern methods such as hatha yoga and t'ai chi will help your coordination, as they are methods for integrating the hot and cold systems. But keep in mind that both hatha yoga and t'ai chi are only optimal when you understand their core philosophies and principles. Otherwise it is like pedaling a bike with your hands, it will get you there, but the feet would be much more effective—you will be repetitively performing these methods mechanically without giving your mind the intellectual framework to practice earnestly.

Another routine that should become part of your exercise schedule is a "deloading phase." Deloading is a practice used in athletic and strength training. It is essentially a rest week, or a scheduled reduction in exercise volume. According to the editors of *Essentials of Strength Training and Conditioning*, "the purpose of this unloading week is to prepare the body for the increased demand of the next phase or period."[12]

A deloading phase will help niggling injuries and mitigate the risk of exercising too much. It allows the body and mind to heal because we are not engaging in any intense exercise or rigid routine. It's about taking one step backward to take two steps forward.

Making exercise a habit is essential. The more we nourish this fundamental through consistent exercise, the more chances we have for experiencing the scientifically verifiable effects of exercise on the mind.

Science

Periods of intense exercise allow the body to naturally function without *thinking* disturbing the process. When we exercise for extended periods of time, especially aerobically, we enter a state of intelligent spontaneity, an effortless state of mind. At the beginning of intense exercise we are fighting this activity because our cold system is analyzing the stress being put on the body. Laziness is an inability to push through this pain threshold, but if you are willing to push through, you will discover this state.

The sense of a controlling "I" in the cold cognition begins to disappear as the automatic functions of the body (hot system) naturally take over. Naturally, parts of our body that are not needed during intense exercise begin to shut down. Energy is distributed to those parts of the body that are necessary. As a result, the cold cognitive regions within the prefrontal cortex are disengaged. Intense exercise essentially downregulates the cold system in a way similar to meditation. If you push through your cold system's angst with intense exercise, the hot wisdom of the body begins to take over, which puts you in a state of intelligent spontaneity.

Neuroscientist Arne Dietrich has researched these cognitive effects caused by exercise. He coined the term "transient hypofrontality," which refers to the phenomenon of how the cold system's downregulation occurs during exercise. Dietrich explains some of the effects:

> Some of the phenomenologically unique features of this state such as experiences of timelessness, living in the here and now, reduced awareness of one's surroundings, peacefulness (being less analytical), and floating (diminished working memory and attentional capacities), are consistent with a state of frontal hypofunction. Even

abstruse feelings such as the unity with the self and/or nature might be more explicable, considering that the prefrontal cortex is the very structure that provides us with the ability to segregate, differentiate, and analyze the environment.[13]

The more consistently we exercise, the better chance we have of entering intelligent spontaneity, which is healthy for our cognitive abilities. It is the same with meditation. Our minds begin to be clearer and more sensitive. Aerobic exercise actually changes our gene expression. Research explains that this has something to do with certain chemicals in our brain that are turned on during exercise. Increased levels of a crucial protein called brain-derived neurotrophic factor (BDNF) are produced during exercise. BDNF allows our brain cells to communicate with each other in a far more efficient manner. This leads to mental calm and clarity, the mind's response to feeling optimal health and well-being. The great feeling we have after exercise is due to BDNF being turned on.

The exercise fundamental is simple: we are at our optimal level of performance when we exercise consistently. It's not rocket science. Exercise is not only essential for our productivity, but also for how we rest. It is important for nourishing the most overlooked fundamental: sleep.

Sleep

In the growing world landscape of excessive busyness, reducing our hours of sleep is considered a sort of badge of honor verifying our commitment to whatever it is we do. The result of such actions is that we feel a subtle sense of stress and anxiety that we assume is normal. Stress and anxiety are common mental problems when we are too busy and not well rested.

We stay on digital devices late into the night after a long day at work. We then rise early and try to recharge by taking a hit of coffee. Generally we believe that we need a coffee in the morning to wake up and get the day started. But the truth is if you just wake up and need some sort of stimulation to get the day started, then you are just tired and need to prioritize your sleep better. When you have a good night's sleep you will be fully awake and alert to tackle the day ahead.

Our society is under the illusion that sleeping less leads to more productivity. People pride themselves on getting less sleep. Many people sleep less than six hours and believe that this is responsible and a way to get ahead. Nothing could be further from the truth. If you are not getting the recommended seven to nine hours a night, then you are less effective during the day. This sleep-deprived suboptimal state has been revealed in epidemiological studies. Matthew Walker, scientist and professor of neuroscience and psychology at the University of California, Berkeley, explains this suboptimal state in his brilliant book *Why We Sleep*:

> Based on epidemiological studies of average sleep time, millions of individuals unwittingly spend years of their life in a suboptimal state of psychological and physiological functioning, never maximizing their potential of mind or body due to their blind persistence in sleeping too little. Sixty years of scientific research prevent me from accepting anyone who tells me that he or she can "get by on just four or five hours of sleep a night just fine."[14]

More importantly, sleeping less than seven to nine hours a night (known as *short sleeping*) has long-term implications on our health and well-being. More than twenty large-scale epidemiological studies tracking millions of people over decades report a loud and clear message: the shorter you sleep, the shorter your life. As a result, many diseases and deaths in developed nations, such as heart disease, dementia, diabetes, obesity, and cancer are causally linked to a lack of sleep (though it's not the only factor, it is a big contributor). Walker explains these health issues:

> Routinely sleeping less than six or seven hours a night demolishes your immune system, more than doubling your risk of cancer.

Insufficient sleep is a key lifestyle factor determining whether or not you will develop Alzheimer's disease. Inadequate sleep—even moderate reductions for just one week—disrupts blood sugar levels so profoundly that you would be classified as prediabetic. Short sleeping increases the likelihood of your coronary arteries becoming blocked and brittle, setting you on a path toward cardiovascular disease, stroke, and congestive heart failure. Fitting Charlotte Bronte's prophetic wisdom that "a ruffled mind makes a restless pillow," sleep disruption further contributes to all major psychiatric conditions, including depression, anxiety, and suicidality.[15]

The old maxim "I'll sleep when I die" may unfortunately come sooner rather than later if you are not getting sufficient sleep. Consistently getting a healthy night's sleep keeps us running at an optimal level. In good humor Walker has an advertisement in his book explaining an "amazing breakthrough" about the health benefits of good sleep:

> Scientists have discovered a revolutionary new treatment that makes you live longer. It enhances your memory and makes you more creative. It makes you look more attractive. It keeps you slim and lowers food cravings. It protects you from cancer and dementia. It wards off colds and the flu. It lowers your risk of heart attacks and stroke, not to mention diabetes. You'll even feel happier, less depressed, and less anxious. Are you interested?[16]

Sleep is underrated in our self-interest-driven world. What is the point of being busy and socially successful if you are not physically and psychological healthy? Often our busyness and resulting tiredness don't allow us to enjoy the great life we have. Busy people are usually snappy because they are just tired, they are sleep deprived. The hot system's tired emotional response is proof that the body and mind need sufficient rest.

We cannot operate at our optimal potential if we consistently neglect our sleep, especially if we are trying to perfect a skill. Sleep acts as a bridge between cold and hot cognition, shifting new memories to brain circuits operating below the level of consciousness. Healthy sleep, in part, allows a skill to become second nature and effortless (nonrapid eye movement [NREM] sleep acts as a magical memory-saving device, as it remarkably saves those memories that are important, especially a motor memory for a new skill). A combination of repetition and consistent sufficient sleep helps new memories (motor or knowledge based) become ingrained skills/knowledge. Sleep has to become a priority if we are to optimize our lives.

For all of those super-busy people out there, being busy all the time is not a badge of honor. Being busy all the time leads to all sorts of problems professionally and personally. Busyness often occurs from multitasking and trying to do too much (along with assigning ourselves unnecessary tasks to make ourselves look busy). The mind is foggy and can't see clearly; it's not sure about the next step. When you have sufficient deep sleep you prioritize your day better.

Without sufficient sleep all the other fundamentals suffer. You will not have the energy for exercising, meditating, or sticking to a healthy diet. Without good rest you will cut corners to try to fulfill whatever you think your busyness is asking of you. As a result we become lazy and neglect the fundamental things that matter. We are too tired to exercise because without good sleep you lose your vigor for the ordinary things that matter. Our exercise routine might be reduced or disappear altogether.

Trading sleep for busyness also affects our diets. We find ourselves lacking the motivation to make a nice wholesome salad, for example, and instead fall into bad habits such as seeking instant nourishment like junk food. Sleep deprivation affects our food choices. Matthew Walker and his research team conducted a study on how people's brains acted with regard to their food choices when they lacked sufficient sleep. They discovered that the thoughtful judgment of the prefrontal cortex was silenced with insufficient sleep, and the more deep-brain regions, those that drive motivations and desire, were amplified.

Walker and his team discovered that high-calorie foods were more desirable to those who were sleep deprived. Our cravings for heavy carbs, sweets, and salty snacks are all amplified (we've all surely experienced this phenomenon). Another contributing factor is that when we have insufficient sleep we have increased levels of endocannabinoids (chemicals produced by the body that are very similar to cannabis) circulating in our body. Essentially with less sleep you get the munchies in the same way you do when you use marijuana. With healthy sleep these chemicals won't affect you or cloud your food choices. You will be motivated and more conscious about what you put in your mouth.

Meditation also suffers from poor sleep. Super-busy people often understand the benefits of meditation but can't really meditate due to the habit of their mind being whisked around like scrambled eggs. There is a growing trend for super-busy/successful people to experiment with meditation techniques. They usually steer clear of subtle deep transformative techniques such as vipassana because they don't want to blunt their aggressive behavior. They tend to gravitate toward methods such as Transcendental Meditation (TM) because it can briefly calm the mind on and off for a twenty-minute period. But even techniques such as TM can be a struggle if you don't consistently get good sleep. An unrested and agitated mind is suboptimal.

No form of meditation will be deep if you're a super-busy person. It is essential to relax at night and prioritize your sleep to meditate well. With consistent deep sleep, your morning meditation will be deep, and as a result you will begin to reap the rewards from *truly* meditating. Deep sleep every day is essential for our lives to flourish. We need to cultivate methods that make sleep a priority.

Prioritizing Sleep

Prioritizing sleep requires a commitment to habits and methods we follow daily. Our ideal time for sleep depends on our chronotype. Colloquially there are two chronotype tendencies: "morning larks" and "night owls." Both likely evolved because of co-sleep as families, couples, or even an entire tribe. Night owls would stay up to 1:00 or 2:00 a.m., on watch, and then sleep in. Morning larks, on the other hand, would go to sleep early and wake up early to accomplish daytime tasks. Yet in the modern world, most of us don't have to deal with the real-life danger of a lion stalking the tribe, so night owls probably don't have to stay up so late, but there is still a difference between the two types.

Our ideal bedtime, then, varies from lark to owl. For a lark between 9:00 and 10:00 p.m. is ideal. For an owl somewhere between 11:00 p.m. and 12:00 a.m. is best. (But please don't try to fool yourself into believing you're an owl just so you have an excuse to stay up late at night. If you are naturally tired earlier and rise early, then you are a lark, not an owl.)

You should begin a process for nourishing deep sleep hours before you lie down in bed. Late nights—according to one's own circadian rhythm—should be avoided by both larks and owls because they inhibit the following day. If we hit our target time, then the next day will most likely be productive and satisfying. As Benjamin Franklin famously said: "Early to bed and early to rise, makes a man healthy, wealthy, and wise." We could take this to mean early in the sense of both larks' and owls' circadian rhythm—9:00 for larks, 11:00 for owls.

Sadly, our world has not catered to the night owl because of the common belief that the early bird gets the worm. Luckily, companies such as Nike and Google are breaking this trend. Both have established more flexible working schedules catering to both larks and owls, matching an individual's circadian rhythm.

The timing of your dinner and what you eat are also important. If you are aiming for my recommended bedtimes for morning larks and night owls, then your last meal of the day should be between 6:00 and 7:00 p.m. for a lark, and between 8:00 and 9:00 p.m. for an owl. This timing allows the stomach time to break down the food and settle your mind as a result. The problem with eating too close to bedtime is that your stomach will be stimulated, and this will subtly agitate the mind and also increase your resting heart rate, affecting your chance of deep sleep.

Having exotic food that stimulates your stomach will surely affect your mind. Eating a spicy curry at night is going to produce a lot of heat in your body, which in turn will agitate your mind. Chili is a no-no. Too much heat will keep you up to all hours of the night, tossing and turning. As someone who loves Indian food, I've experienced this on many occasions. One notable mention was when my wife and I spent four months in Tiruvannamalai in India's southern state of Tamil Nadu (my favorite place in India, maybe the world).

I'm a big fan of a southern Indian dish called *dosa*, especially masala dosa. One night my wife and I went to a local restaurant we had never been to before and ordered two masala dosas. I don't think either of us have eaten anything hotter in our lives, and my wife is from South Korea so that says something (Korean food is like fire). As I was eating my dosa the heat from all the spices, especially the chili, were making me dizzy to the point that I thought I was going to have a panic attack. My body was internally hot for about eight hours, and my mind was racing. As a result my sleep was terrible, and the next day I paid the price on the throne (toilet), a painful experience. So don't do anything stupid like me and have spicy food at night. (Indians usually have dosas for breakfast for obvious reasons.)

Eating a high-carbohydrate diet is also problematic for good sleep. A careful study of healthy adults monitored a four-day diet high in sugar and other carbohydrates but low in fiber. This study resulted in the adults having less deep NREM sleep and more awakenings at night.[17]

It is best to have plain and simple food for dinner. Embrace a wholesome salad or nutritional vegetable soup at night. Eating a plain and simple dinner hours before bedtime will help nurture deep sleep.

The food we eat is important, but what is as important is the input we take in through our eyes and ears throughout the evening. Many people are in the habit of using digital devices in any spare moment they have, especially at night. At night people want to chill out by watching television; surfing the internet on a computer, laptop, tablet, or phone; or basically playing with their phone all night. Though we may feel chilled out, we are not truly relaxing. We are really relaxing when we cease activity. Stimulating our mind through the input we take in through the eyes and ears is still activity, as we are stimulating the sympathetic nervous system (SNS). The mind is being agitated by sensory input. To truly relax means to stop a lot of sensory input and allow the mind to just settle in this present moment.

It's perfectly fine to be bored. The feeling of boredom comes because we are used to filling our mind full with digital junk. The only way to feel less bored, and for the feeling of boredom to diminish over time, is to embrace boredom. Don't be afraid to examine your mind and find out why you are bored. This examination will reveal the sensory input our mind has become accustomed to. If we don't learn to embrace boredom, then we will continue to fill our mind up every day with sensory noise. This has disastrous effects on our sleep. Using digital devices at night stimulates the SNS too much, leading to disorders such as insomnia. Actually, research explains that one of the main contributors to insomnia and restless nights is the blue light in digital devices.

We've all experienced a restless night's sleep after we have stared at our phone, television, or laptop just before bed. Some of us have evolved to stare at our phones while we are in bed. The scientific research of the blue light's effect on our mind reveals a connection between bad sleep patterns and digital devices. The blue light in digital devices depletes our pineal gland, a pea-size organ in the brain. The pineal gland is a primary organ for facilitating a good deep sleep. A few hours before your regular bedtime, the pineal gland begins to release melatonin (a hormone that regulates biological rhythms), which reduces your alertness and makes sleep more inviting. But exposure to blue light keeps the pineal gland from releasing melatonin, which ultimately messes with our circadian rhythms, affecting our sleep patterns and causing us to remain alert and ready for action as if it is daytime.*

Ancient Chinese thought correlates to modern scientific thought on this matter. The Chinese concepts of yin (feminine/passive/cold) and yang (masculine/active/heat) are important in this correlation. In Chinese thought the circadian rhythm of nature fluctuates between the yang energy of daytime and the yin energy of nighttime. Daytime is for active work while nighttime is for resting and recuperation. When we engage in yang activities at night, our mind becomes agitated and ready for action.

Yang activities at night mess with our circadian rhythm as our mind assumes it is the beginning of the day. Mental yang activities are worse than physical in this instance. Exercise at night is better than none at all, though not as good as in the morning because, as I previously mentioned, body temperature can remain high for an hour or two after physical exertion, making it more difficult to fall asleep. But mental activity at night, such as being engaged in lengthy conversations or using digital devices, are what throw us out of balance. The Chinese perspective of yang activities at night causing restlessness is an ancient explanation as to why blue light suppresses melatonin production. To counter this digital bombardment we need to cultivate healthy habits to eliminate nightly stimulation.

One such method is *digital sunsets*, a phrase coined by philosopher and optimal life coach Brian Johnson. Digital sunsets consist of shutting down all digital devices, including turning off your phone, by 6:00 p.m. at the latest, but preferably 5:00 p.m. for maximum benefits. The next time you turn on your digital devices is when you begin your work the following day, not before.

---

*For more on the relationship between sleep, the pineal gland, and blue light see the following articles: Atul Khullar, "The Role of Melatonin in the Circadian Rhythm Sleep-Wake Cycle," Psychiatric Times (website); Harvard Health Publications, "Blue Light Has a Dark Side," Harvard Health (website); and Heather Flint Ford, "Seeing Blue: The Impact of Excessive Blue Light Exposure," Review of Optometry (website).

Associate professor of computer science at Georgetown University and anti-social-media advocate Cal Newport applies this approach to his life. At 5:00 p.m. every day after addressing all his emails and other matters, he shuts his computer down and finishes the workday by stating "shutdown complete." This end of workday mantra symbolizes that he has truly finished his work for the day and won't see another digital screen until the following workday. The digital sunset approach allows him to be more present with his family at night.

Digital sunsets allow us the time to enjoy each other's company again, without the interference of a digital device. Talking face-to-face is far better than chatting on social media. Digital sunsets also address the blue light issue. It is a great method for curing insomnia and correcting poor sleep patterns. Digital sunsets enhance melatonin production and as a result enhance health and well-being.

On top of all these methods for prioritizing sleep is a nightly cocktail that acts as a sleeping pill. It's really more of a tea than a cocktail. I learned this from social entrepreneur Tim Ferriss, and he in turn learned about it from the late, great Dr. Seth Roberts. The cocktail consists of two tablespoons of apple cider vinegar and one tablespoon of honey (I use raw organic forest honey), stirred into a cup of hot water. My wife adds chamomile for extra impact. If you drink this cocktail thirty to sixty minutes before bedtime, you will surely be knocked out. The funny thing is that there is no research as to why this drink has this effect, but it works. Ferriss was a lifelong insomniac, and this cocktail contributed to curing his poor sleep patterns. I've tried both hot and cold versions, and they work equally well.

All of these methods and tips I've shared will help you sleep more deeply, consistently. The result of consistent deep sleep is that it gives the three other fundamentals the required energy they need to function optimally. Once our four fundamentals function optimally as one, creating the foundation for masterpiece days, we begin to bear the fruit of growth on our way to peak performance.

5

CULTIVATE
INTELLIGENCE AND
HARNESS CREATIVITY

By following the four fundamentals we stay grounded while our chances of developing skill and reaching peak performance are enhanced. The fundamentals can be thought of as the rich soil that nourishes the fruit of learning and creativity. Using them to create masterpiece days sharpens our learning capabilities and emotionally intuitive sense of creativity and helps them to function optimally. The little things do matter. Meditation, nutrition, exercise, and great sleep build the bedrock for future success.

Often people want to learn and be creative, but they can't focus for long periods of time and have no creative calling. This is common in our world today because we are so distracted. A mind constantly distracted will only seek more distraction because it is used to overstimulation. A distracted mind is like the ocean waters during a hurricane. On the other hand, a tranquil mind is like a pristine lake on a bright and sunny day. A motionless lake is transparent and reflective; you can see right down into its ultimate depth. The four fundamentals of a masterpiece day facilitate such depth of mind. Our attraction to entertainment is destroying our innate ability to learn and be creative. Constant entertainment pacifies our mind. As a result intelligence is undervalued in our world, and creativity is thought of as something isolated to artists. The truth is eclipsed when we overfeed our mind with entertainment and poor food, forget to exercise, and just allow our thoughts and emotions to run amok. We become desensitized to the world around us and even ourselves, as we vicariously watch the whole world implode into unconsciousness.

Earnestly following the four fundamentals reconnects us with the world and most importantly our inmost selves. Becoming more conscious of our inner and outer landscape allows us to learn and create at an optimal level. However, developing expert skill and reaching peak performance also depends on having the discipline and dedication for cultivating more intelligence and creativity, which will enhance your overall life. The irony is that many people who just go through life with no discipline and allow life to push them around are often arrogant about what they "think" they know and are incapable of learning as a result. They have not been humbled by life, so they continue to fight and be jaded. We are unable to learn when we are rendered unconscious by overstimulation of body and mind.

The Seeker's Mind

Cultivating intelligence requires us to finally admit that we don't really know anything. This is not a desirable position to be in in our world. We always want to save face by appearing to be intelligent. We often speak about topics and current affairs that we really don't know anything about because we are paranoid that not knowing about something opens us up for criticism. But it is highly unintelligent to speak on matters we don't really know about. Even current affairs are issues we shouldn't speak about. Just because the news broadcast or newspaper gives us information on certain matters doesn't mean we actually know what's really going on. It's unintelligent to formulate opinions on such scarce information without diving deep into the subject. Following the four fundamentals uproots this tendency.

By nourishing the little things in our life we realize that we actually don't know much, but on the flip side we are eager to learn. As a result we are not afraid to admit that we don't know because that is the most honest and intelligent position to be in. We learn to be truly humble and not at all worried about not knowing, and as a result we approach life as explorers rather than know-it-alls. We embrace the seeker's mind, meaning we remain a student of life. Having a seeker's mind cultivates intelligence, which allows us to grow psychologically. Our minds become more articulate and clear, which becomes evident in our speech and emotional conduct. If we pretend we know, we cannot learn. And if we cannot learn, we cannot grow. Learning is the fertilizer for growing our intelligence. Learning is just like nature because it is nourishing, moving, and growing—it's alive! Learning itself grows our mind, and if we are growing, then we are fully alive.

Our habit to try to be a know-it-all cuts us off from the feeling of growing and being alive. Once we think we know something categorically we stagnate and disconnect from our mind's natural growth. Our all-knowing habit makes us come across as an authority on certain matters, but we forget that information always changes and knowledge deepens as our mind grows. By remaining a student and continuing to learn throughout our lives, we understand more and continue to grow. Even when we think we aren't learning, life is teaching us, as philosopher Jiddu Krishnamurti explains:

> There is no end to education. It is not that you read a book, pass an examination and finish with education. The whole of life, from the moment you are born till the moment you die is a process of learning. Learning has no end and that is the timeless quality of learning.[1]

There should be no end to learning. If you are humble enough to remain a student your growth will be continual, and as a result your mind will cultivate a keen intelligence that has a deep understanding of self, others, and life. This process should continue to the day we die, as Mahatma Gandhi said, "Live as if you were to die tomorrow. Learn as if you were to live forever."

Learning nourishes this deep intelligence, making us more aware with a profound sense of understanding. Deep intelligence is something we all can have if we are willing to do the work. If you follow the four fundamentals and continually learn without arrogance, then it is yours. We are losing contact with intelligence because of the toxic habits that keep us distracted. Instead of diving headfirst into distractions, we need to go old school with simple habits that have become background noise in our modern world.

Reading as a Discipline

Reading books is essential for learning. Books are a super fuel for cultivating intelligence. But in our modern world books have taken a backseat to the toxic habit of watching screens. We watch television and watch on our smartphones and computers. It's a constant observation of everybody else's lives but our own. When we watch whatever it may be, including mindlessly surfing the internet and scrolling the social media feeds, we zone out in a stupefied zombie state. As a result, watching too much stuff on screens makes us stupid.

Watching screens doesn't require a lot of our attention. The more we partake in watching activities the less our mind can concentrate and think clearly. When people have these types of habits it is hard for them to complain about their lives. How can any of us complain if we are not making our lives conscious?

We need to take our power back. Instead of watching stuff on screens mindlessly, we need to turn to reading books, preferably physical books. Turn the act of reading into a discipline. Reading itself requires an ability to focus for extended periods of time, so a daily discipline of reading cultivates focus and concentration. As a result we have an improved ability to focus and concentrate that can be applied to anything. So buy a bookcase and fill it full of books. Not fiction books, but nonfiction books on philosophy, science, religion, art, and so on. To cultivate intelligence you need to tackle the big subjects that will give you a clearer understanding of life.

Make your reading discipline a daily ritual. When it is time for digital sunset, switch over to a physical book. I like to read at least three hours a day, usually after digital sunset, but if I'm not writing in the morning I will read then. Extended periods of reading are similar to meditation. Your mind is focused on reading, and as a result you enter a state of effortlessness, where time disappears. The added bonus of this is that at the same time you are cultivating intelligence.

The evidence that reading makes you more intelligent can be found in your expanded vocabulary. Your ever-growing vocabulary enables you to be more specific in conversations and writing, so you can articulate ideas in a way people truthfully understand. This ability is what attracts us to intelligent people, who are usually well read. Comedian and actor Bryan Callen is a voracious reader, and he inspired illusionist David Blaine to read more. As he explained to Blaine, "The difference between the people you admire and everybody else is that the former are the people who read."[2]

We should not neglect our ability to be more intelligent. The key is to remain a student without becoming clever. Even if you believe you know something categorically, that understanding will likely change over time and you with it. We are better learners when we nourish the four fundamentals, but we are also more creative as well. The more we cultivate intelligence, the better creators we will be.

Nourish Creativity

Taking care of all the little things in our life contributes to a mind more capable of being creative. Following the four fundamentals and cultivating intelligence nourishes our creative faculties. Many creative people are disciplined and don't waste time with distractions; a distracted mind hinders creativity.

We would assume Hollywood director, screenwriter, and producer Christopher Nolan is a pretty connected guy technologically, given his popularity. But he is quite the opposite. Even though Nolan has created such epics as *Interstellar*, *Inception*, and the recent Batman trilogy, he's done it all without a mobile phone or email account. All of his energy is dedicated to his work. Anything else distracts him from a pure creative process. The question you need to ask yourself is this: Are all of the gadgets and gizmos I own enhancing my creativity or distracting me from it?

I am often shocked that a lot of people own a television, desktop computer, laptop, tablet, and smartphone. This sort of super connectivity is not natural, and it causes a lot of subtle anxiety and destroys any chance we have of being creative in any way. There is no reason any of us need so many gadgets.

Personally I only own a laptop. When I was living in South Korea in 2013 I purchased a phone for job opportunities. I tried to purchase a push-button phone but sadly realized that South Korea had stepped far beyond that technology, so I reluctantly bought a smartphone. It was a pure headache for me. Hearing the sound a phone makes when a message is received or when it rings is pure torture. I'm used to peace and quiet, and I'm not used to people depending on me to answer the phone or return a message. Thankfully, in early 2014, I moved back to Thailand and that phone has become a good camera, minus the beeps, tweets, and what have you.

For my writing to be at its best my mind needs to be uncluttered. I cannot have the sense of ever-impending doom brought on by the sound of a phone distract me. And to get the best out of my writing, I write a book by hand first; yes, pen and paper. Then I type it up on my laptop, but I definitely don't turn the Wi-Fi on during this process. Turning the internet on while in a creative process is like throwing bait out there to distract your mind. My creative process is not something new; it's what any committed artist has followed for a long time. It's a trusted method. The difference between, say, da Vinci and myself (besides the level of genius, of course) is that the world I live in is full of distractions. If you're not disciplined and committed to your skill, your creativity won't survive.

Avoid Attention Residue

Research also backs up the point that distractions destroy creativity. Sophie Leroy, a business professor at the University of Washington Bothell, explains in a 2009 paper intriguingly titled, "Why Is It So Hard to Do My Work?," an effect she called *attention residue.* The effects of attention residue are simple: when we place our attention on something other than our task at hand, it forms a lagging residue that affects our ability to focus on our original task, especially if the other things we moved our attention to are not finished tasks. For example, say that you plan to sit down to write after breakfast, but before breakfast you check your emails and read some that require a reply but put off dealing with them until later in the day. Those unaddressed will linger in your mind, affecting your creative output when you write.

Another classic example is having a lot of tabs open in your browser while you are typing and trying to concentrate on your work. This causes your concentration levels to drop because the open tabs are like mind bait, enticing you into unnecessary distraction. Even if you briefly interrupt your work to check your social media or email, it will cause attention residue and hinder your work when you return to it.

Attention residue is one of the main reasons we are becoming a less creative species. We can't continually distract our minds with frivolous nonsense, such as scouring a person's Instagram images, and be creative at the same time. You have to choose one or the other. Are you committed to cultivating skill and reaching peak performance? Are you all in? Or are you just all talk and only interested in zoning out in front of a digital screen?

We have to be fully committed to developing skill and reaching peak performance, as we cultivate intelligence and harness creativity along the way. To be the best version of ourselves we need discipline and commitment, not distraction. To be more creative we need to be mindful of the effects of attention residue. To nourish the creative process we must stay away from all distractions. Building a masterpiece day is not only done by following the four fundamentals and finding time to cultivate intelligence; it also relies on time dedicated to undistracted creativity.

Time Blocking for Deep Work

Creativity itself, like reading, can be a discipline we follow daily. We need a commitment to a daily creative process, and to get the best out of it, we need to remove all distractions from our day. To achieve this we require undistracted time blocks. Time blocking is a method practiced by many world-class performers. The way it works is that you block off a certain amount of time each day that you dedicate toward your creative work. Time blocking allows you to go deep because you are not distracted. Newport calls this *deep work*. He explains that deep work involves "professional activities performed in a state of distraction-free concentration that push your cognitive capabilities to their limit." He also says that "these efforts create new value, improve your skill, and are hard to replicate."[3]

Consistent daily time blocks for deep work will enhance your creative skill. Many creatives, though they may not know or use the term *deep work*, follow this method of daily time blocking to further hone their skills. We need those daily hours to go deep to become more skillful on our way to peak performance.

When I was writing this book, I followed a similar method. From Monday to Friday I would sit down from 8:30 a.m. to 12:30 p.m., when the creative juices would flow the best. That four-hour time block would only be altered every second day when I would skip going to the gym in the morning and would start writing at 8:00 a.m. One other reason that block might be altered is if I made lunch for my wife and me, in which case I would stop writing at 11:30 a.m. But 90 percent of the time that four-hour window is nonnegotiable, and I will be at my desk grinding away and trying to deliver the best book that I'm capable of.

Undistracted time blocking will allow you to nourish your creativity as you continually go deep. Three to five hours a day is best for deep work. Anything less than three hours is okay because it's better than nothing, but the problem with fewer hours is that you are not pushing yourself beyond your limits, where there's a lot of the gold to be mined. Personally I believe four hours is best, but you could stretch that to five hours if you feel like Superman. But going beyond five hours is not beneficial. Trying to do too much causes burnout, and when you are overworked you lose all momentum going forward.

For example, when I first began writing ten years ago I used to have monster sessions. I would write sometimes for twelve hours without lunch or basically any break. The problem with long sessions is that you become extremely anxious and even dizzy from being in your head all day. As a result you often need a few days off to recover. All of your previous momentum is lost. Our mental faculties have a daily limit, and if you exceed those limits, your energy reserves will be depleted. We want to push but not deplete. If you have no energy the day following a big session, then you are depleted.

If you follow the three-to-five-hour time blocking rule, then you won't ever be depleted. The upside of this is that you build momentum. For example, if there was a race between a time blocker and a long sessioner to finish writing a book first, who do you think would win? The momentum of a time blocker carries them forward to win easily because there are no breaks in their routine, and they do not experience burnout. When our energy is not depleted, we have the vigor to press on with clarity and precision. Time blocking allows our creativity to flow undistracted.

Deep-Work Schedule

Honing our skills cannot be achieved if everything outside our creative process is a mess. To fully harness creativity we need to develop a daily schedule for masterpiece days, of which our creative time block is a part. We must stay true to the four fundamentals and cultivating intelligence. Deep work, as with exercise, is best to do in the morning.

When you begin your day positively, everything else just falls into place. And even on the off chance that things go wrong later in the day, you deal with them better because you have already achieved what you set out to do for the day, so there is no anxiety. I recommend that you choose earlier in the day for time blocking. The way you structure your day around that is as important as the task itself. Below I share with you my schedule for writing this book, which you could use as a template to follow or tinker with to suit your requirements.

6:00 a.m. — Wake up

6:15–6:45 a.m. — Meditation

7:00–7:45 a.m. — Exercise

8:00–8:25 a.m. — Breakfast

8:30 a.m.–12:30 p.m. — Deep-work time block

12:30–1:00 p.m. — Stretch and check emails and social media

1:00–1:30 p.m. — Lunch

1:30–5:00 p.m. — Downtime with my wife

5:00–5:30 p.m. — Follow-up emails

5:30–6:30 p.m. — Digital sunset

6:30–7:00 p.m. — Dinner

7:00–9:00 p.m. — Read books and meditate

9:00 p.m. — Bedtime

There are plenty of spaces in my schedule for unexpected variables. My time may not stick to the letter of the law, but I do my best to follow this schedule when I'm writing a book. Having a strict schedule is always best for when you have a certain project that needs your extreme care. I am mindful that my circumstances are quite unique compared to someone who works an average eight-hour day or has children to care for every day. But this should not deter you from creating a schedule around your working hours and family commitments.

For example, if you are a morning lark and go to sleep at a decent time there should be ample time to meditate and exercise in the morning. As for a deep work time block, if you are not fortunate enough to work at a job that is your passion and inspires you to go deep, then your time block could be in the evening, perhaps during your time of digital detox. Instead of watching TV or surfing the internet at night, go deep into something that inspires you creatively. You might not be able to have a lengthy time block, but even if you can spend one hour a day on deep work that will surely build momentum over time.

Downtime is also important in our day; otherwise we become robots with no room for error or fun. My wife and I like to visit temples, go for walks, meditate in nature, enjoy good food, or even watch a movie or sporting match. Without downtime we don't enjoy the fruits of our labor. We become primarily cold system creators without the hot system's spontaneity or fun. Though I have explained the benefits of discipline and structure for skill and peak performance, allowing life to spontaneously happen and just have fun are also important for our health and well-being.

Obviously, each individual's situation is different, but when we create a schedule based on the four fundamentals and time for deep work, that allows us to cultivate skill and move toward peak performance in whatever it is we choose to do. A scheduled framework for masterpiece days nourishes creativity and energy, and an optimal life is born from the creation of masterpiece days. As a result we can transform our days to be more productive as we continue to reach the best version of ourselves. All we need is a complementary operating system to go with it.

Philosophy as Your New Operating System

When people hear the word *philosophy* they often imagine a bunch of weird people who sit around waxing lyrical about the universe. Though that surely exists, it is pretty far from the general truth. Philosophy has nothing to do with posturing—intellectual or otherwise. Philosophy is a love and dedication to wisdom.

If you are a philosopher in the truest sense of the word, then you are dedicated to studying wisdom and becoming wiser as a result. But even if you don't consider yourself a philosopher, we all need to commit our lives to studying wisdom and being wiser. We need more wise people in the world. Many of us have certain operating systems that we perceive and judge the world through. This builds biases that we are not conscious of because we've stopped growing. As you've probably recognized, we don't need more subjective viewpoints in the world, we need a lot less. A seeker, on the other hand, is consistently growing, as they show a healthy skepticism for absolutes.

When we harness the seeker's mind, we upgrade our old operating system with a new one centered on intelligent growth. Philosophy is that operating system. By studying philosophy you don't become a fundamentalist and stick to one point of view. On the contrary, you see the benefits in all belief systems and how they apply to your life in a pragmatic way.

The amazing thing about philosophy is that it allows you to explore other subjects with clarity. Studying Eastern philosophy primarily for the majority of my adult life has made it easier and also more appealing to study psychology, culture, religion, art, and evolution. You actually gain a greater respect and understanding of things such as religion because you understand the benefits they have for the mind and society. Uploading philosophy to your operating system allows your mind to be more subtle, where you are more aware of your own internal landscape and also the world and life in general. Cultivating intelligence requires the nourishment of philosophy. Having a philosophical bent will make you more intelligent, adaptive, and receptive to new information entering your consciousness.

In short, you will be wiser, and the wise are the true leaders in our world even though this doesn't appear true at times. The wise are those who help human civilization evolve because they have the intelligence to be trusted.

When we begin our training, it is important to follow the four fundamentals, harness creativity, and cultivate intelligence with our new operating system. But one of the most important things we need to transform is our lifestyle. The next chapter is focused on an ancient lifestyle method that will complete our training for achieving optimal performance.

6

FASTING THE MIND

To train ourselves efficiently to reach peak performance, we must transform our lifestyle in a radical way, so our mind is able to be productive without mental activity overwhelming us. Thus far, all the training methods I have shared, from vipassana and Zen meditation techniques to the four fundamentals and cultivating intelligence and harnessing creativity, are disciplined aspects of a much older lifestyle method known as *fasting the mind* or *mind fasting*.

The practice of fasting the mind is spread across ancient Eastern thought, including the Advaita Vedanta tradition in Hinduism, the practice of vipassana in Theravada Buddhism, and open-awareness meditation in Zen Buddhism and through the Taoist sage Chuang-tzu. Actually, the phrase "fasting the mind" comes directly from Chuang-tzu when the Chuang-tzu text is translated into English.

There is a passage in the Chuang-tzu text where Confucius as the master and Yen Hui as the student are in dialogue about a corrupt ruler in the state of Wei. Usually Chuang-tzu does not have a completely favorable opinion of Confucius's philosophy, but in this passage Confucius plays the mouthpiece of Chuang-tzu, as Confucius was the most popular teacher during the Warring States period of China. In this particular passage Yen Hui has devised many schemes to try to make the ruler of Wei benevolent and compassionate toward his people, whom he has neglected for far too long. But Confucius is not at all convinced by his plans. He feels that Yen Hui is trying to influence the ruler with his own beliefs. After shooting down many hatched schemes, Confucius has had enough and explains to Yen Hui that as long as he is filled with such subjective opinions and beliefs about how the ruler should change, it will actually cause more trouble:

Confucius said, "Goodness, how could that do? You have too many policies and plans and you haven't seen what is needed. You will probably get off without incurring any blame, yes. But that will be as far as it goes. How do you think you can actually convert him? You are still making the mind your teacher!"

Yen Hui said, "I have nothing more to offer. May I ask the proper way?"

"You must fast!" said Confucius. "I will tell you what that means. Do you think it is easy to do anything while you have [a mind]? If you do, Bright Heaven will not sanction you."

Yen Hui said, "My family is poor. I haven't drunk wine or eaten any strong foods for several months. So can I be considered as having fasted?"

"That is the fasting one does before a sacrifice, not the fasting of the mind."

"May I ask what the fasting of the mind is?"

Confucius said, "Make your will one! Don't listen with your ears, listen with your mind. No, don't listen with your mind, but listen with your spirit. Listening stops with the ears, the mind stops with recognition, but spirit is empty and waits on all things. The Way gathers in emptiness alone. Emptiness is the fasting of the mind."

Yen Hui said, "Before I heard this, I was certain that I was Hui. But now that I have heard it, there is no more Hui. Can this be called emptiness?"

"That's all there is to it," said Confucius. "Now I will tell you.

You may go and play in his bird cage, but never be moved by fame. If he listens, then sing; if not, keep still. Have no gate, no opening, but make oneness your house and live with what cannot be avoided. Then you will be close to success."[1]

Confucius advocates for Yen Hui to listen with his spirit. What this means from a contemporary standpoint is that the cold cognition, referred to as "mind" in the passage, has downregulated, and the hot cognition is accessed through a deep embodied state of presence and unwavering mindful awareness.

The term *qing* in Chinese is used by Chuang-tzu in the text referring to a mind (cold cognition) that has been fasted away. Qing has a few meanings. It can mean "facts," "emotions," or, with regard to the Chuang-tzu text, "species-specific essence." The Chuang-tzu interpretation of qing is drawn from Mohist logical theory.* To give a few examples of qing as a species-specific essence, think of the uniqueness of how a horse's gallop is like no other and how a cobra can stand vertical and hiss like no other snake.

Qing is a characteristic that defines a species. But with human beings Chuang-tzu believed that our qing is actually a flaw. According to Chuang-tzu, our species-specific essence is our ability to discern between "this" and "that" in our mind (cold cognition). This ability leads to subjective viewpoints of right and wrong, good and evil, likes and dislikes, and so on. As a result we build a partial view of the world based on our conditioned perception and beliefs. Qing, then, is the separate and isolated state of "I," which is who you believe you are. We approach our lives with partiality by doing so, and as a result, we cannot contribute to the world without having a deep-down agenda.

Fasting the mind is a practice and lifestyle focused on uprooting our agendas, either conscious or unconscious ones. When we fast the mind,

*Mohist logical theory is part of Mohism. Mohism was an ancient Chinese philosophy during the Warring States period based on logic, rational thought, and science developed by academic scholars who studied under the ancient Chinese philosopher Mozi.

we lose our qing, or in other words downregulate our cold cognition. As a result we bring the intelligent spontaneity of the ingrained hot system to life. We essentially have freedom from our ego's discernment of how the world should be according to its habit of mentally labeling everything "this" and "that." Chuang-tzu explains in the text how a sage is not affected by qing:

> The sage has the outward physical appearance of a human being but lacks human essence. Because he looks like a human, he flocks together with other people. Lacking human essence, though, he does not allow right or wrong to get to him. Lowly! Small! In this way he belongs to the world of humans. Elevated! Great! Standing alone, he perfects his Heavenly qualities.[2]

The "heavenly qualities" in this passage refers to the deep spontaneity of the hot system. Those qualities come alive when we have no qing. This was Confucius's point in the fasting the mind passage. He knew Yen Hui was intoxicated with qing, so he recommended fasting the mind. Yen Hui had no chance of changing the ruler with his partial view. He needed to become impartial, allow life to be as it would without qing getting in the way. Only from that state of consciousness, as Chuang-tzu explained, can Yen Hui succeed.

By downregulating cold cognition we feel a greater sense of unity with life—"make oneness your house" as Confucius explained. We become almost like a limb of the universe, with a connected feeling to everything. As a result, our attitude changes because we feel as though we are part of something much greater than ourselves. When we get out of our subjective self-interests we are more selfless. When we are out of our own way, our view is more holistic. Cold cognition is analytical, while hot cognition is a natural faculty for perceiving holism because nature is holistic.

The analytical perspective of cold cognition is what we believe is beneficial for oneself and society. But this view is relatively new around the world and was not always shared. In the East, as we discover with Chuang-tzu, many deep thinkers were skeptical of analytical thought. In fact, the evolution of both the analytical mind and holistic mind were environmentally determined. Psychologist Richard E. Nisbett explains:

> The ecology of China, consisting as it does primarily of relatively fertile plains, low mountains, and navigable rivers, favored agriculture and made centralized control of society relatively easy. Agricultural peoples need to get along with one another—not necessarily to like one another (think of the stereotype of the crusty New England farmer)—but to live together in a reasonably harmonious fashion. This is particularly true for rice farming, characteristic of southern China and Japan, which requires people to cultivate the land in concert with one another. But it is also important wherever irrigation is required, as in the Yellow River Valley of north China, where the Shang dynasty (from the eighteenth to the eleventh century B.C.) and the Chou dynasty (from the eleventh century B.C. to 256 B.C.) were based. In addition to getting along with one's neighbors, irrigation systems require centralized control and ancient China, like all other ancient agricultural societies, was ruled by despots. Peasants had to get along with their neighbors and were ruled by village elders and a regional magistrate who was the representative of the king (and after the unification of China, of the emperor). The ordinary Chinese therefore lived in a complicated world of social constraints.
>
> The ecology of Greece, on the other hand, consisting as it does mostly of mountains descending to the sea, favored hunting, herding, fishing, and trade (and—let's be frank—piracy). These are occupations that require relatively little cooperation with others. In fact, with the exception of trade, these economic activities do not strictly require living in the same stable community with other people. Settled agriculture came to Greece almost two thousand years later than to China, and it quickly became commercial, as opposed to merely subsistence, in many areas. The soil and climate of Greece

were congenial to wine and olive oil production and, by the sixth century B.C., many farmers were more nearly businessmen than peasants. The Greeks were therefore able to act on their own to a greater extent than were the Chinese. Not feeling it necessary to maintain harmony with their fellows at any cost, the Greeks were in the habit of arguing with one another in the marketplace and debating one another in the political assembly.[3]

It's no surprise, then, that a lot of holistic philosophy is attributed to Eastern thought. Naturally the cultivation of rice required people to be less self-interested and more centered on what was best for the group. Selfless individuals contributed to the greater good.

Though times have changed, the holistic view of Eastern thought is making a comeback into popular consciousness. The difference with the modern social landscape is that when we are selfless in our path we ironically bring value to the world. Our expert skill becomes an extension of the universe, and we bring value to the world through the inspiration we provide by reaching peak states of performance. Instead of your work just benefiting yourself, it more importantly benefits the world. This is holism in action.

We feel a great sense of connection to the world when we give ourselves totally to our chosen path. The sacrifices we make and dedicated discipline we have for our path evokes a humble selflessness. We cannot progress when we are lazy and self-interested. Some may financially succeed in business by being aggressive and self-interested, but that attitude only enhances their ability to be an asshole. And I'm not interested in your becoming an asshole but rather someone who is humbly at their optimal level of potential, which will bring value to the world. To live a peak-performance lifestyle we must focus on our skill rather than being driven by money. Let money come once you've achieved success in your skill.

Eliminating distractions, even your yearning for wealth, will allow your skill to shine. Fasting the mind allows intelligent spontaneity to run wild, bringing your uniqueness and value to the world. But we must not succumb to the distractions our mind often seeks.

Distraction Detox

Intelligent spontaneity is embodied when we are committed to our skill and focused on eliminating the distractions that take our attention away from it. When you follow the practice and lifestyle of fasting the mind, you are making a commitment to keeping your mind peaceful. A peaceful mind is a fasted mind, meaning you are free of distractions.

We usually allow our mind to go unchecked in its hunger for absorbing distractions, but we have to be mindful of this habit. We might not be able to do this 100 percent of the time, but our commitment to eliminating distractions should be nonnegotiable. This commitment is easier to achieve when we follow our disciplined approach of the four fundamentals. Keeping the daily practice of masterpiece days motivates us more to drop distractions. Periodic detoxes from certain distractions are beneficial. Some distractions, on the other hand, can be dropped altogether. A detox from distractions allows our mind to fast, so it can heal at a deep level and also bring our skill to life.

Reduce Digital Consumption
In chapters 4 and 5 I discussed the practice of digital sunsets. This practice is a no-brainer if you want a peaceful and more productive mind. Reducing your digital consumption is imperative to fast the mind. Constantly being on digital devices affects our mind at the subconscious level, leading to bad habits and anxiety.

We often don't assume digital consumption causes bad habits and anxiety, but it does. This occurs because the SNS is overly stimulated from digital consumption. This causes latent habits and anxiety to become ingrained within the subconscious, and these become our unconscious reactions toward life. If we continue to overuse digital devices our minds will become deeply damaged on a cognitive level.

Our minds are adapted to nature, not anxiously scrolling the social media feeds, which is like crack cocaine for our eyes as it subtly depletes our nervous system as drugs do. We all feel exhausted when we've been on a digital device for too long. Some people try to push the limits, as we see with PC gamers in South Korea who go on such lengthy gaming sprees that there has been a growth in adult diaper sales. But this unnatural attempt to stay on digital devices for too long has led to mental health issues and even deaths. As a result there are internet addiction centers popping up all around the world. We don't need things to get to this stage.

We need strategies to counter the effects of digital use. Effective strategies must be focused on minimizing our digital use. One such method is allocating a certain time of the day to check the internet. This should not be before breakfast as that type of habit will set the day in a negative direction. Ideally you want to schedule your internet time after your deep work time block in the morning.

For example, I don't check my emails or social media until 12:30 p.m., and usually only for thirty minutes. This thirty minutes is what I call my "management period," as I address emails that need to be taken care of and discuss with my wife, who handles the media side of my work, things that I need to jump on before they get out of hand. I have another thirty-minute management period before my digital sunset at 5:30 p.m.

One hour a day is overly generous for me, and I'm sure you could shoot for probably less than that, as I know I could. Again, keep in mind I don't have an active phone, tablet, or television, so my laptop is my only active digital device. Along with reducing your time on digital devices, you should also strive to reduce the quantity of your devices. We need to remember that we lived for hundreds of thousands of years without digital devices, so we actually don't need them, but they do come in handy for communication and learning.

The problem is, as with many things, we don't practice moderation with our consumption. Preferably you should strive to have only one device. A home computer, either desktop or laptop, is best. And if you're paranoid about having a mobile phone, it's best not to have one. But if you need a phone for work, then revert back to one designed only for calls and texting.

Petter Neby, an entrepreneur and founder of the Swiss consumer electronics company Punkt. (period included), which is the German word for "full stop/period," has created many products designed to keep our focus, such as a slick push-button phone that only texts and calls. A technological return to retro is important if we are to live less distracted lives, as Neby explains:

> Today's world is consumed with technology and I think we are too distracted by it in day-to-day life. I founded Punkt. to offer a viable alternative for those feeling overwhelmed by the advanced technologies that have pervaded modern lifestyles. Punkt. is about using technology to help us adopt good habits for less distracted lives.[4]

Neby also shares his concerns regarding how modern technology is distracting us from the real world:

> I think the "always on" life is probably even worse than having a poor diet. Every day we are consuming more trash, and becoming more detached from real life and the ability to deal with situations head-on. Just look around, it's a disaster—and the sociological issue of our times.[5]

Sell your smartphone, and feel the open space within your mind. As for televisions and tablets, nobody needs them. A television is a great waste of space. With all the spare time you could gain by refusing to watch television, you could put a bookshelf in its place and fill it full of books that are going to contribute to your intelligence and peace of mind.

Minimizing your digital devices and reducing your daily digital consumption will allow your mind to breathe and be spacious without succumbing to the habit of filling it full of frivolous information and entertainment. This method is enough to detox your mind from the distraction of the digital world, but many people's daily digital consumption is so high that it requires a complete digital detox for an extended period of time.

A long period of digital detox is very beneficial for fasting the mind, essentially healing it as a result. Spending a week to a month or two away from digital devices is where you'll feel the greatest benefits. Your mind becomes crystal clear, ideas come effortlessly, and you have a greater sense of unity with life. Walking becomes a joy, just walking. Listening to the insects and birds is like music to your ears. Listening in conversations is much deeper. Everything slows down.

These simple things that we are not conscious of in our super-busy lives are the bedrock of life that we come back in contact with. A spacious mind is creative, eager to learn, peaceful, and awake. Reducing our digital consumption is a fast-track method for fasting the mind and becoming an optimal performer.

No More Gossip

Gossip is so common in our world. It's hard to find a conversation that is not centered on it (or I should say centered on somebody else). Gossip is plainly a bad habit. With the advent of digital devices in the information age, we often know too much about things that don't really matter. We hear about a Hollywood couple's breakup and speak about it as if we know them personally. Our bad habit of watching screens fuels our need for gossip.

It gives me a psychosomatic headache to hear people *always* talking about other people behind their back. Are our lives so boring that we have nothing better to do? The irony is that those people we usually gossip about are famous people dedicated to their skill in the hope of one day reaching perfection. Everybody is human, and we make mistakes at times. But their dedication to their skill is why they are the source of gossip and not one of the crowd.

If you strive to live a peak-performance lifestyle through cultivating expert skill, then your attitude should be focused on being in *front* of the crowd rather than a part of it. To be in front of the crowd means you have no time for gossip because you're focused on yourself. When we worry about what others are doing, we forget about what we should be doing. Gossip is a waste of the precious time you need to reach your optimal potential.

If you are a gossiper and your friends are also gossipers, then the chance that those same friends gossip about you is a high probability. It's ironic, isn't it? While you are happy gossiping about other people, it's highly likely somebody else is doing the same about you. How do we break this chain of gossip?

We need effective strategies to curb our habit of gossiping. Begin with the obvious steps: stop watching news programs, entertainment gossip shows, or any show that could cause a need to gossip to your friends. I never watch the news or read newspapers. People think this is strange and ignorant on my part, but they couldn't be further from the truth. When big and important news actually occurs, I hear about it without the news shows, newspapers, or social media because it is the course of everyone's conversations and concerns. I've followed this practice of not listening to or reading the news for ten years, and the world is still here doing its thing. The world didn't end because I refused to watch the news.

It's also important to remember that much of the information and news we get is not all that significant to our own lives. For instance, why is it important for us to know that Angelina Jolie and Brad Pitt broke up? People break up every day. Why should we need to know about their private lives? Wouldn't it be better to give them the privacy we would want and refrain from parroting the gossip the news feeds us? Say no to the programs fueling gossip.

Another more skillful strategy can be used when we meet up with our friends. When the conversation begins to lean into gossip, change the subject or inquire into how their lives are going. This method becomes refined over time, as we learn how to transition into another topic smoothly.

The habit of speaking about other people will distract you from your commitment to reaching your optimal potential. Ceasing gossip altogether makes you more positive and allows your mind to focus on what is really important. You become clear on what your goals are.

Don't Be Cynical

Gossip and the all-round habit of speaking about other people not in your presence leads to cynicism. A cynic has a pessimistic outlook on life. We all fall into the trap of being cynical at times, especially when we strongly disagree with the attitude of others. There are unscrupulous people in our world that surely deserve our contempt, or at the very least our disapproval; for example, a leader who drops bombs on innocent people, an evangelist who extracts money from gullible religious followers, or anyone who hatches any sort of scheme to rip good people off. But the problem with entertaining cynical views is that it becomes a habitual way of framing our conversations. As with gossip, the majority of conversations are laden with cynicism. An unhealthy diet of verbal cynicism is a main contributor to the negativity bias that has evolved in our brains. Psychology offers a definition of negativity bias:

> The negativity bias refers to the notion that, even when of equal intensity, things of a more negative nature (e.g., unpleasant thoughts, emotions, or social interactions; harmful/traumatic events) have a greater effect on one's psychological state and processes than do neutral or positive things.[6]

Negativity has this powerful effect on our mind. Though a negative experience might be brief, it will often crowd out all the positive experiences. For example, say a family goes on a seven-day holiday and everybody is having a great time. Every day just keeps getting better, and the kids and parents are loving it. But on the last day the parents get into a heated argument. This argument dampens the mood on the way home, even though 99 percent of the holiday was fantastic. This is negativity bias in action.

That one-minute situation is what our mind focuses on. All of the great experiences are forgotten. But it actually doesn't have to be this way. Fasting our mind and training ourselves to appreciate the fundamentals give us a clear picture of what is happening. We can view the situation objectively as a momentary blip where we lost ourselves. As a result we choose the positive reaction of forgiveness and an ability to discuss it without emotion, which actually heals the problem, and then we remember the positive experiences more. The sooner you address the situation the better. Avoiding the situation just allows emotions to fester, which contributes to unwanted resentment.

Addressing the negativity bias and its cynicism requires a commitment to being a more positive person. Just ask yourself how you feel when you are negative and cynical. None of us feels great. Being positive enhances growth, while negativity and cynicism stunt it—though this shouldn't mean we become a full-blown Pollyanna. Pollyannas are often overly optimistic even in situations where there is no room for optimism. Trying too hard to be a Pollyanna comes across as fake, and we all can sense it. The skill is to be optimistic without being foolish. You maintain a sense of realism, and if it is required, you can call a spade a spade.

But more often than not we don't have to be cynical or negative. Both have become a habit we feel comfortable with. Sometimes we choose to be cynical because it feels comfortable, which is stupid. If your commitment for reaching your optimal potential is strong, then being genuinely positive is a prerequisite. Pessimists usually don't change the world; optimists do. Optimists change the world because they keep their mind open to the possibilities around them. Pessimists, on the other hand, usually close down from the world around them because all they see is grim, dogged existence. If life is a grim, dogged existence for you, then you have no chance of developing skill and reaching peak performance.

Many successful people have a positive outlook. This attitude contributes to their success. Being optimistic allows you to fulfill your potential. Instead of falling into self-doubt, realize that your life is moving in a forward direction; it is just a matter of gaining control of the reins so you stop being pushed around. Being pushed around by life is often our fault, because our pessimism fuels our self-loathing and our habit of giving up too easily. When you say no to cynicism and train your mind not to be the victim of the negativity bias, then optimism will grow in you. Your renewed positivity toward life will build an attitude fit for an optimal life. Get used to it and thrive.

Eliminate Multitasking

With our modern busy lives, we believe it is beneficial to multitask to get ahead. Nothing could be further from the truth. The general rule of thumb among successful people who live optimal lives is that they go from finishing one task to starting another and don't try to do more than one thing at a time. Our natural mind is analog, not digital. It is not overly equipped for multitasking. We can multitask, but it causes subtle anxiety and ultimately distracts our mind too much, to the point that sometimes when we are trying to do a lot of things at once, we don't achieve anything.

Doing one task at a time builds momentum. You finish one project thoroughly and move on to the next one. You might have a job that demands multitasking, but you can navigate through this anxious terrain intelligently. You need to prioritize your time well. You need to pinpoint which project is the most important and what one task will make the rest easier. These types of strategies diminish the effects of multitasking. All in all you should be striving for this one foot after another strategy.

In the end you will be more productive and learn a lot more from not being bombarded by multitasking distractions. We are accustomed to multitasking because sometimes distracting ourselves takes us away from the important task at hand. People will be in their office with all of their social media pages open while they try to concentrate on their work. Good luck! That bait is too enticing, and people often find themselves shuffling between social media and their actual job. As a result they don't get much work done at all.

Usually the one who is most effective and productive with their work doesn't easily fall for the bait of multitasking. They are experts at eliminating distractions and curbing their urge to distract the mind. They crowd out all distractions that compel us to multitask. As a result they can remain focused for extended periods of time. We can all do this, but we need to cultivate habits focused on one thing at a time. By starting with the small things we can effect great change.

For example, when people exercise they often listen to music through their headphones or watch something on a screen. In this case the mind is seeking distraction from the physical stress of exercise. But you are actually causing yourself anxiety on a subtle level because you are multitasking and making it far more difficult to focus on the single task at hand. Instead of listening or watching something when you exercise, just exercise and feel the pain. Focusing on the physical stress of exercise will strengthen your mind. Focusing on one task at a time strengthens your mind because you cease the habit of seeking distractions.

Another example is our use of the internet. We are accustomed to the bad habit of listening to something and reading something on another website at the same time. For example, we've all experienced watching something on YouTube and then thinking of something else to check, such as an article. As a result we end up reading the article while the YouTube video is playing at the same time. We hear the audio, but we are reading something entirely different. Our attention might be focused on the article, but our mind is still processing the audio. It's hard in this instance for the mind to discern what it should focus on. Our mind is essentially fragmented.

The stress this puts on the mind is too much, and a big reason we feel depleted after using the internet. Our sensory input is overwhelmed, and sensory overload leads to chronic anxiety and panic attacks and affects our productivity and sleep. We are not a computer; we cannot manage multitasking efficiently, and we are causing more harm to our mind than we think. Make it a habit to focus on one thing at a time when you surf the net.

Applying these few strategies will positively influence your professional and everyday lives, making you more productive. Multitasking is a technique of distraction that the mind easily falls prey to. Say no to multitasking and reclaim your power.

Wake-Up Rituals

Waking up in the morning is tough for the best of us. We might have had a restless sleep, and when the alarm goes off it feels like a jumbo jet is weighing us down. Or we might have eaten a heavy carb dinner the night before, which makes us sluggish in the morning, and we reach for the snooze button. But we can counter such habits with rituals that do take some time to master.

The first obvious method is to prioritize your sleep the night before, eating a light meal a few hours before sleep, practicing digital sunsets, drinking some apple cider vinegar with honey, and going to bed on time (methods I mentioned in chapter 4, The Four Fundamentals). Prioritizing sleep should make it easier to wake up on time in the morning, which will make it easier to deal with the bad habits we are guilty of from time to time.

Not getting enough sleep and cultivating laziness through bad diets and no exercise are the main bad habits we fall into. In Zen training in many Zen Buddhist monasteries they practice immediately rising out of bed. When the alarm goes off you jump straight into action. I have found that prioritizing sleep helps this habit form. If I prioritize my sleep I have no problem rising immediately and sometimes actually wake up before my alarm goes off. Immediately rising out of bed can be a difficult practice to master, especially if you've had a terrible sleep. But even with a terrible sleep it is possible.

In the Zen tradition they go through periods of fasting the mind with intense meditation called *sesshins*, a Japanese word that means "touching the heart-mind." A sesshin requires us to go to bed at 10:00 p.m. and to wake up at 3:00 a.m. The day is full of numerous meditation sessions (each thirty to sixty minutes long and anywhere from nine to fifteen periods a day), general duties such as cleaning the monastery and keeping everything in order, and a few small vegetarian meals a day, and the retreat is strictly silent, meaning no talking at all. This goes on sometimes for seven days and even longer in some extreme cases. But somehow, like well-trained soldiers or a samurai, at 3:00 a.m. they jump out of bed to tackle the day. This very deliberate practice trains the monks' minds not to wander in laziness upon waking up. The alarm acts as a whip cracking them into action.

The mind tends to wander as soon as it wakes up, and the way it wanders is usually through fantasy. When people first awaken, they often fall into the habit of fantasizing about sex and other pleasurable circumstances such as being extremely wealthy. To start the day well we need to stop this habit. Training the mind not to wander when we wake up is very important, especially if we want to put our best foot forward for the day ahead.

In the Theravada Buddhist forest tradition of Thailand they aim to eliminate this habit by practicing mindfulness as soon as the alarm goes off. Stabilize yourself, be aware of the mind wandering into its own delusions, and watch all fantasies disappear under the mental gaze of mindfulness. These few wake-up rituals can help us to lead more optimal lives, but they are even more potent when they are combined with long periods of mind fasting.

Drop Off the Map and Bliss Out

All of the distraction detox methods are great for transforming your lifestyle, as they keep the mind fasted in the busyness of society. They help you manage your life and transform your habits for optimal performance. But the problem you will discover is that you may still be playing out the ingrained patterns of your culture. Though your habits may have changed, you may not have experienced any real transformation on the deepest level.

This is where the long mind fast is essential. People who travel extensively and stay away from their home country for years understand this on a superficial level. Ethnobotanist Terence McKenna explained in a lecture that dropping ourselves into a completely different country for an extended period rewrites our hardware (subconscious). I can testify to this, as I have spent the majority of my adult life in Asia away from my birth country of Australia.

I actually don't feel very Australian at all (whatever that means). Don't get me wrong, I still enjoy watching the odd game of NRL and exploring the outback and beaches (if that's what it means to be Australian). But for better or worse, I don't share the same concerns or have the same habits as a lot of Australians. I believe this comes from my life in Asia, practicing and studying the Eastern traditions, along with the fact that colonized Australia is a very young culture (my hope is that the real aboriginal history of Australia becomes ingrained in the culture and is eventually taught in schools).

Though vagabonding for years will have this subtle effect on your cultural programming, it is not an efficient long-term mind fast because you are still in contact with *a* culture and society. A long-term mind fast requires us to drop off the map altogether. It is designed to keep your mind away from any sensory input for an extended period of time— usually between two weeks and six months every year. One month is ideal, but if your schedule doesn't allow that much time away, two weeks is also effective. It's also important to have a particular location that you go to every year for this mind fast. Preferably you should choose a location away from your country that has a different culture, so you don't easily fall back into familiar cultural habits or see any friends you know. The location should be close to nature and quiet.

On these long mind fasts it is important not to have any digital devices with you, including a standard television and radio. This means no internet at all. Also, no alcohol, drugs, or processed foods and junk foods should be consumed. You should eat as "cleanly" as possible. An idea for this period, in true Eastern fashion, is trying to avoid meat since the average person eats too much of it. Daily meditation and speaking as little as possible are prerequisites. Physical exercise is not as important during the long mind fast. The reason is that during the long mind fast we don't want a lot of stress on the body. We want to give it an extended period of time to heal from any little niggling injuries or strains (recall the deloading phase from chapter 4). Walking is enough during this period.

Temporarily renouncing the world and your normal life has permanent effects on the mind. During this period, instead of continuing our habit of overstimulating the SNS, we activate the PSNS more often, which leads to deep states of relaxation and subtle states of unassociated ecstasy. This subtle ecstasy in India is referred to as *blissing out*. We bliss out when we stop striving and quell our volition. In the East blissing out all the time is imperative for sagehood, and there is nothing wrong with that because a lot of wisdom comes from that peaceful place. But unless you want to be a sage, a two-week to six-month mind fast away from your volition and striving is plenty to be therapeutic.

Temporarily ceasing your habit of doing and instead just being is extremely beneficial. Just *being* is important in the long mind fast. Tuning out society to bliss out is what allows us to appreciate life itself minus the distractions that color it. This bliss is different from happiness, as our happiness usually depends on people, events, situations, things, and so on to make us happy. This bliss is at the end of striving and association; it's naturally there but eclipsed by our habits and distractions. Just a short period of two weeks away from the world and your normal life will reveal it. But the longer you stay away from the distractions of the world, the better chance you have of bringing this bliss back into your ordinary life in society.

For the past few years I have scheduled an annual long period for fasting the mind. My preferred location is Tiruvannamalai. I rent a house outside of town in nature, not far from where a lot of sadhus congregate around the Hindu holy mountain of Arunachala.

In the past I've been able to do a mind fast at this particular location that lasts for four months. But with the evolution of my work, this is no longer feasible. So I try to schedule two weeks to a month in Tiruvannamalai to fast my mind and regenerate. Tiruvannamalai is a primarily Hindu town, so I revert back to a clean vegetarian diet. I meditate a lot more than usual daily, anything from vipassana to qi gong. I usually read a famous Eastern text to center my mind throughout the day but try not to read too much. The only exercise I get is a long walk to buy a young coconut from my local friend who climbs coconut palms all day, and then usually after that I will visit my two friends who are brothers that sell the best masala chai in town. Spending a super slow month away from my "normal" life has permanent deep effects on my whole way of life, not to mention my mind.

The long period of fasting the mind transforms the patterns that define who we are. The transformation is so deep that it is possible we will rewrite our subconscious. This all depends on our effort in the long mind fast and how much time is allocated to it. It is a commonly held belief that it takes twenty-one days of repetitively doing something before it becomes an ingrained habit. But in just fourteen days the long mind fast can implement long-term changes to the patterns that define us. All of these fasting-the-mind methods for detoxing distractions allow us to examine our character and the person we have become.

Breaking Mental Patterns

The lifestyle method of fasting the mind allows us to reach the best version of ourselves. But the irony is, as with the downregulation of the cold cognition, the best version of ourselves is devoid of a strong sense of self. The more egotistical we are the less chance we have of developing skill and reaching peak performance. Paradoxically, the more humble we are the better chance we have at succeeding at our skill. The humble person usually doesn't have a strong sense of self. So the more we let go of who we think we are the more we become who we ought to be. As a result, the East questioned the nature of the self. What is it? Who are we? The discoveries they found are astonishing and have universal implications now more than ever.

Hinduism, Buddhism, and certain Chinese schools of thought are in agreement on an important revelation regarding the self: a person is a temporary bundle of mental patterns and ruts that they are repetitively caught in but can change at any time. The existence of a permanent person with a certain natural mental structure is a misunderstanding of who we are, though keep in mind some Eastern traditions have differing beliefs with regard to the existence of a soul. Nevertheless, both of these ideas exist beneath the mental person.

As a result of these patterns and ruts that we repetitively fall into every day, we say such things as, "I'm just an angry person," or "I'm a fearful person," or "I don't like when they do that," and so on. These do not really describe who we are but instead are patterns we continually exhibit. Nobody is naturally angry; anger is just an existing pattern a person is comfortable with when dealing with familiar situations. Consequently, an individual's emotional response becomes predictable if you know that person well enough.

While we obviously have a lot of patterns that are harmonious, the problem is that we also have a lot of patterns that are negative and keep our lives from progressing. These patterns and ruts are embedded so deep within us that we incorrectly assume they are who we are, that they are part of our nature. The extreme no-fuss mentality of Eastern thought maintains that if these patterns are not who we are, then shouldn't there be a way to break them? And if we break these patterns, won't we be more authentic and develop more positive patterns? The East's answer is a resounding yes! It is not only possible but something that all of us should strive to do if we want inner and outer peace. But the difficulty about this endeavor is that a lot of the repetitive patterns we play out daily are on a subconscious level. They are essentially a software virus implemented in our hardware.

But as with computers, this is not a death sentence, and it can be fundamentally changed with the right system. In the ancient East, as a lot of traditions began to evolve and share ideas, many technologies were developed. One such technology was a psychological framework followed in three of the main Hindu philosophies of Vedanta, Samkhya, and classical yoga, a system we could call *Eastern psychology*.

This psychological framework is made up of three elements: *samskaras*, *vasanas*, and *karma*. The Sanskrit term *samskara* means "mental impression" or "subliminal imprint." Samskaras are the power-base of the subconscious. Everything we have endured in our life from the time we were infants is recorded in the subconscious. Actually, many of our patterns were developed during infancy. Our subconscious (samskaras) houses the patterns that we believe we are, and it is because of the fact that these patterns live on a subconscious level that makes them so hard to break.

These subconscious patterns drive our vasanas, or habitual ways and latent tendencies, and together, our patterns and habits drive our actions, or karma. *Karma* literally means "action," and in this regard our actions are unconscious because they are driven by our habits and patterns within the subconscious. Our mental patterns define our actions, and the majority of the time our actions are unconscious. So the dilemma is, how do we uproot our patterns if they are on a subconscious level that we cannot actively reach to transform them?

To fundamentally change our patterns we need to begin with our actions. Instead of acting unconsciously in predictable ways, be mindful of your actions. Earlier I mentioned the Sanskrit terms *viveka* (discrimination) and *vairagya* (nonreaction). Both of these are essential tools for the process of transformation. When we are more conscious of the actions and emotions that get stirred up and compel us to act, we can cease our patterned response. So when you get stirred up and feel an urge to act, practice nonreaction.

As I mentioned earlier, meditation will help this nonreactive practice to become a habit. We are actually training the body (hot system) not to engage with certain spontaneous emotions and sensations in situations that reinforce those patterns. This Eastern psychological framework is similar to modern cognitive training, the purpose of which is to change our latent habitual tendencies.

Training our actions transforms our habits. When our actions change, our habits and tendencies follow suit because we have cut off the habits' drive that fuels our actions. When our habits and tendencies begin to change and become more subtle, we then begin to transform the patterns wound up in our subconscious. As a result new patterns can begin to form in the subconscious that drive more harmonious habits and actions, making us more pleasant people to be around.

Eliminating existing patterns can actually reduce a lot of the anxiety and stress we suffer from. The reason is that when we succumb to the same old patterns that cause us to suffer, we feel anxiety and stress for not having the strength to overcome them. But by following this Eastern psychological approach to fasting the mind we fundamentally transform the patterns that you mistakenly took for who you are.

Breaking the patterns that don't serve you is essential if you want to have an optimal life. We need to fully realize that the self, the sense of "I," is just a bundle of interwoven patterns that only define who we are when we continue to fall into their repetitive trap. The lifestyle practice of fasting the mind, along with all the training in part 2, is about eliminating the excessive baggage in your life that is weighing you down from reaching your full potential.

Developing skill and reaching peak performance requires you to be a humble student. And it is hard to be humble when you let mental patterns hijack your life. Who you are is not this "person" with all these problems, emotional responses, habits, and so on. Who you truly are is the best version of yourself that you are waiting to become. Apply this optimal training, and experience your peak state of performance.

PART 3

Optimization

7

THE NATURE OF
PEAK PERFORMANCE

Optimizing and actualizing your potential depends on understanding the science of skill and peak performance along with strictly following the four fundamentals of masterpiece days. Both evoke an optimal experience. But what is that experience like? How do we consciously know we've entered states of peak performance? How do we know intelligent spontaneity has taken over? First and foremost, our attitude must be committed to optimization. Reaching peak states of performance is impossible without dedication.

Our commitment to cultivating skill by following the four fundamentals is the seemingly unrelated key to experiencing states of peak performance and eventually living out a peak-performance lifestyle. The commitment we show toward creating masterpiece days and cultivating skill determines our ability to be in a state of peak performance spontaneously. This means our skill is so ingrained that it is a response of intelligent spontaneity, and as a result it has become a part of you, almost like an extra limb.

There is no distinction between who you are and your skill. Your skill is analogous to the aroma emanating from a flower. Your skill was wound up inside of you, just like the aroma was within the flower, and all the hard work and dedication has brought your expert skill forward to inspire the world. All of our hard work and dedication is what takes us to champion status. Talent is great, but it is useless without steely determination. As a result states of peak performance are dependent on determination, not talent.

Training our hot cognition extensively will eventually evoke the naturalness of intelligent spontaneity. Yet even though you might be highly skilled with an ability to be in a flow state of intelligent spontaneity, the experience is short-lived if you don't continue to grind away. If you believe you have reached the mountaintop, then you will stop growing and not refine your skill. Peak performance states depend on experiencing intelligent spontaneity more often, to the point that it is natural. And it's no surprise that reaching peak performance requires steadfast dedication to the four fundamentals and deep work.

Leading sports psychologist Jim Afremow explains that the average performer practices until they can do something right, and the elite performer practices until they can't get it wrong. It's just a slight change of mind-set, and that small change is the big difference between those who are just great and those who are true champions. Those obsessed with practicing to the point of getting nothing wrong are those who experience peak performance. Cultivating skill to the nth degree ingrains it completely in the hot system, to the point of naturalness. The naturalness of peak performance actually feels like the world is getting slower. This is a real cognitive phenomenon world-class performers' experience.

Perceiving Reality in Slow Motion

Reaching peak performance through the naturalness of intelligent spontaneity allows us to sense reality in slow motion, where overthinking and overanalyzing have ceased. Everything slows down, and as a result effective action can be taken. A state of peak performance evoked by intelligent spontaneity makes the world feel slow, as our skill responds effortlessly to whatever is required.

In the film *The Matrix*, Neo (played by Keanu Reeves) has a martial arts program downloaded into his mind. But even though the downloaded program has taught him the skills, he has had no training. So he is taught by a master called Morpheus (played by Laurence Fishburne). At the beginning of his training Neo couldn't hit Morpheus. Morpheus was too fast for him because Neo was still restricted by the limitations of the "real world" his mind believed in; in other words, his habitual patterns. As Neo's training continued, Morpheus continually advised him to stop *trying* to hit him and just *hit* him, to let go. Essentially, Morpheus wanted Neo to free his mind from the habitual constraints that did not exist in the matrix. As Neo refined his skill, he started to develop this sense of letting go. Instead of applying his cold cognition he was letting go of it (downregulating it/freeing his mind) and allowing the hot cognition to take over. As a result he started to move too fast for Morpheus and proved that he could hit him even though he pulled the blow short of contact.

This letting go of limitations and old habitual thinking extended into all parts of Neo's life in the matrix, where we discover he can now dodge bullets, jump long distances from one building top to another, and so on. UFC fighter Tony Ferguson explains succinctly this relationship between *The Matrix* and the cultivation of skill with slow motion as it applies to his own experience:

> When you're in the zone it's a completely different feeling, you're in the tunnel zone where just nothing else matters. It's like everything's going so fast but you prepared so much that everything slows down. Almost like in *The Matrix*. When you find that flow you get that glow.[1]

Ferguson is a classic example of being committed to the cultivation of skill and the experience of intelligent spontaneity. In the UFC it's hard to find another mixed martial artist who puts in as many hours of hard work as Ferguson. His career is ascending as a result. Some of the greatest NRL footballers of all time, such as Johnathan Thurston, Darren Lockyer, Andrew Johns, and Cameron Smith, all speak about how the game slowed down for them toward the end of their respective careers. Even though they were physically slower on the field, their decision-making abilities were more spontaneously intelligent.

Watching Thurston play during his career, it seemed as though he had all the time in the world on the field, which allowed him to decide the fate of most games in his favor. It doesn't matter whether it is Neo, Ferguson, or Thurston; they all perceive the playing field in slow motion. It is no surprise that just like Ferguson, Thurston was one of the hardest trainers in the NRL even though a champion such as he had accomplished almost everything in the game at such a young age. But Thurston was an elite performer who practiced until he couldn't get it wrong. He was not physically gifted, but his determination for greatness was what set him apart from the pack. His drive was hard to bottle.

Peak performers invariably work the hardest and put the most hours into their training. The effect of slow motion sensory awareness is a cognitive response from repetitively cultivating a skill. The more committed we are, the easier it is to spontaneously see effective solutions. Even though things are happening at a very fast speed, they appear slow to one who is a master of their skill. A sense of slow motion allows a champion to make the right move at the right time, and this ability affects our natural reactions in general and can be adapted to whatever life brings.

The slow tunnel vision effect in our skill allows our decision-making to be more precise. We essentially become more effective human beings. We find solutions to problems easier and are not overcome by the obstacles we face. Our life is naturally harmonious. We move like Cook Ting's blade slicing up an ox. But one of the core debates in ancient China was whether our natural intuitive sense for effective actions and solutions was something endowed or learned or a bit of both.

Natural Spontaneity and Trained Spontaneity

The ancient Chinese sage Lao-tzu would probably refute a lot of what I've said in this book. Though he might agree with me in principle, he might have a problem with training our skill to be natural. Lao-tzu's feeling was that intelligent spontaneity (wu-wei) is naturally intrinsic in doing nothing, and thus everything is done. We could say he was the first hippy. Lao-tzu explains that spontaneous reactions come naturally to us without training. He is not entirely wrong, but to what degree is he right?

As I've explained, intelligent spontaneity is a feeling of naturalness. This naturalness is a commingled concept in Chinese thought, a blending with wu-wei. The concept is *tzu-jan*, which means "spontaneously of itself"; in other words, nature functions in this organic spontaneous manner. And of course, we are nature as well. Lao-tzu's philosophy is that nature is as it is, with natural spontaneity driving it. There is a natural order we align with (the concept of the Tao) that governs the movements of all life. Lao-tzu advocates for us to stop striving to feel this naturalness and find harmony with the world. This type of philosophy is rife in the East; it is shared by the twentieth-century Indian sage Ramana Maharshi among many others.

Such simplicity is imperative for us to discover, as I mentioned in chapter 6, on fasting the mind. But to what length do we follow this approach? Do we renounce the world completely? I advocate two weeks to six months, but Lao-tzu believes it should be our way of life. He is not wrong, as there is no "right" way to live. It's horses for courses. You could be attracted to ultrasimplicity and let life be as it will without actively influencing it, or you could seek to discover this simplicity in your skill to nourish it.

The natural harmony of the universe is an ever-present truth. While Chuang-tzu doesn't disagree, he also says that in complex social designs we need a level of skill to navigate its tricky terrain (hence the Cook Ting story). The natural freedom Lao-tzu explained can be discovered in a life dedicated to whatever we choose. Philosopher Alan Watts explains:

> Spiritual freedom involves much more than going on living exactly as you have lived before. It involves a particular kind of joyousness. . . . It is the discovery that to accord with the universe, one has but to live, and when this is fully understood it becomes possible to live one's life with a particular zest and abandon. There are no longer any obstacles to thinking and feeling; you may let your mind go in whatever direction it pleases, for all possible directions are acceptable, and you can feel free to abandon yourself to any of them.[2]

This level of freedom is a mind not stricken with fear. It doesn't mean fear has disappeared, but rather that we are not mentally crippled by fear when it arises. Our mind is free to follow a life of inspiration and beauty. We don't have to head off into the mountains and become a hermit. The freedom of naturalness is right where you are. Both Lao-tzu and Chuang-tzu are right. We do have natural, inclinations, but we can also be trained, and in a complex world, some form of training is essential. Spontaneity is spontaneity; it is natural, and it is also expressed through training. But as I mentioned in part 1 our natural hot system can make intuitive errors if we don't have a strong cold system.

The two systems in cognitive science explain how spontaneity is both natural and learned. But intelligent spontaneity is a natural function of hot and cold cognitive integration. Our trained skill merges with our raw nature to express the beauty and magnificence of life. The freedom Watts mentioned is discovered not only in life as it is but also in our skill when it has become embodied. We accord with that natural freedom in the same graceful manner as a calligraphy artist does with their canvas. A master calligrapher will brush their strokes effortlessly, not making a single mistake.

Our training can harmonize with nature to unleash the hidden beauty within us that Lao-tzu describes. He is right; we are naturally good (I explain this further in the next chapter), but he is not completely right, especially when it comes to trusting our hot intuitions wholeheartedly.

Our natural actions, reactions, and solutions to a matter can be disastrous if we have not trained our hot cognition to intuitively sense the environment correctly. It might cost us a business deal or friendship or make us irresponsible and emotional in the threat of impending conflict. Natural spontaneity emanates the natural order and beauty of life, but at the same time our spontaneous actions and reactions can bring harm to oneself and others.

Our endowed nature was not designed to deal with the unnatural complex world we find ourselves in. Training spontaneity through a skill is essential to move efficaciously through the world. Such training strengthens our resolve to deal with the inevitable obstacles of life. Many of us react emotionally when we struggle with life, but training spontaneity (cold cognition training hot cognition) allows you to embrace it and as a result overcome it. Your actions and reactions will be centered and focused, allowing your innate goodness to shine on others. An optimal life is a life in harmony with the world. Spontaneous skill evokes this harmony.

Chuang-tzu's philosophy of ingrained skill uncorks Lao-tzu's philosophy of the innate goodness within us, bringing it forward through expert skill. This end goal of training spontaneity is the core philosophy behind martial arts.

A true martial artist desires to take their effortless skill and make it a natural part of them. Being in intelligent spontaneity more often through practice leads to harmonious dispositions in the self. Your effortless skill goes from the superficiality of performance to merge with your hot cognition, affecting your character at its deepest level. Your skill is one with you and begins to permeate your whole life.

An average performer might be able to enter a state of intelligent spontaneity, but the experiences can be sporadic. An elite performer, on the other hand, enters a state of intelligent spontaneity naturally for longer periods of time without trying to do so. This is evident in sports when a champion athlete is in the zone more often than the other competitors. As soon as it's time to perform they can be in the zone as effortlessly as going from one room to another. This is what separates world-class performers from the rest.

The skill is so ingrained in the hot system that the cold system downregulates almost simultaneously when the skill is required to perform. As a result the mind evokes the skill much quicker than those who need time to enter the zone. When a world-class performer's skill is required it comes to them as naturally as changing direction. Expert skill calibrates with the environment (intelligent spontaneity) spontaneously of itself in the same natural way our walking calibrates with the ground. Striving to reach perfection, as an elite performer does, transforms ordinary actions into spontaneously authentic actions that require no thinking or analysis. Training spontaneity transforms our entire nature. We begin to act spontaneously correct.

Intelligent spontaneity itself is evoked from a mind of no deliberation (deliberation is a function of the cold system). A mind of no deliberation is the art of naturalness. Nature is expressing itself from an empty but stable mind. Training spontaneity allows us to respond spontaneously correct without having to think it out (I discussed this in the koan discussion in chapter 3, see page 63). Thinking itself is the opponent of spontaneity.

The art of training spontaneity to be harmonious with the environment is illustrated through ancient Japanese fencing. An aspiring fencing student must first find a fencing master. When the student arrives at the master's home they are under the impression that the master will train them immediately in how to use the weapons. But to the student's shock the master tells them to forget about weapons and learning any techniques and instead concentrate on cleaning the dishes. Every day the student must wash the dishes.

As the student cleans the dishes on their first day, the master comes out of nowhere and hits the student in the head. The following day the student is preparing their defenses for a headshot, and then the master springs from a different direction and lands a blow to the student's ribs. The next day as the student muscles their rib defense, the master gives them a swift crack across the butt. This process goes on for weeks, as the student continually fails to defend against the master's blows. After almost a month, the student realizes that all of their defensive efforts are futile. As a result the student learns to let go of defensive schemes. The student doesn't "think" about what will happen or where the master will come from next.

Letting go allows the mind to be equanimous. This is the naturalness of intelligent spontaneity. This is a state of mind in complete poise, absolute centeredness, and natural spontaneous response. As the student rests in this spontaneous alertness the master comes and swings for a blow to the nose but the student defends it effortlessly, without thinking about it. It doesn't matter which direction the master comes from because the student will defend all attempts without having to plan for them. This is the art of fencing but also the art of life.

The student's absolute centeredness and natural spontaneous response reflect the height of our actions and reactions in peak performance. We respond with clarity and are on point in our actions. Trained spontaneity not only helps us deal naturally with whatever life brings, but it also allows us to trust our actions.

Trust Skill

World-class performers trust their skill and themselves in general. Their confidence comes from the years spent grinding away and their constant ability to reach peak performance. This type of confidence is hard to bottle. It comes from years or decades of training and striving for greatness. But this confidence also comes from having no self-doubt and their ability to just tackle anything head-on. Many people think too much and start to doubt and question their own capabilities. And many are afraid of failing, so they gain no ground.

World-class performers are not afraid to fail, and this is what separates them from the rest. They see failures not as defeats but instead lessons to learn and grow from. Failures actually lead to more confidence because they give us the strength to deal with whatever life throws at us. And if the failures continue to compound on top of each other, it might be a sign that it is time to reinvent ourselves. Sometimes to get better at our skill, to the point of trust, requires an objective view of where we are and where we want to be, meaning what we want to achieve. Having an objective honest opinion about ourselves can lead to the things we need to get better at and change. That uncomfortable conversation with ourselves (introspection) invariably leads to the answers we seek.

If you can't trust your skill or are stagnating in it, then don't be afraid to pull out all the stops to get there. Don't be afraid of stepping out of your comfort zone to reach greatness. Personally I had to learn to embrace what is beyond the borders of my own comfort zone. How could I write or speak with any authority about Eastern thought or its practices if I didn't immerse myself in the culture? You don't go to a chef to learn how to build furniture, and likewise I realized that if I wanted to truly know about Eastern thought, then I needed to surround myself with the people and culture that such rich philosophies came from. I didn't just want to be a well-learned book scholar with no real life experience. I had to continually step outside of what was normal to get to a level in my own skill that I could trust. Everything comes down to how much you want it.

If you have the balls or ovaries to go through the long hard slog in cultivating skill, then we can trust that reaching a state of peak performance is going to happen if we just *apply* ourselves. World-class performers are confident they can reach peak performance if they just get going. They ascribe to the Nike slogan, "Just Do It!" By just doing it, they get a lot done. Even though they may still have performance anxiety, they just get on with it and have no doubt. They trust their skill.

Novelist Paulo Coelho is a good example of trust in skill. Coelho has written many novels, most notably, *The Alchemist*. When Coelho writes he usually procrastinates a little in the morning, but then he makes a decision to sit down and write with an attitude of "see what happens." He doesn't particularly know what he's going to write because he's not a big note taker. He just trusts that if he at least sits down, then the writing will come, and it does. World-class performers don't ask questions when it's time to perform. They just trust their skill, and intelligent spontaneity is evoked as a result. As a writer, I know that just by sitting down at my desk the words will come to me, even if it does take some time.

This trust in skill promotes a high degree of confidence. For example, a champion athlete might be behind on the scoreboard, but they don't get flustered. They trust their own ability to get out of any situation, and more often than not they succeed in doing so. They trust the right solution will come because they trust their own abilities. By trusting their skill, they enter intelligent spontaneity and reach peak performance. And even if you aren't a world-class performer it's better to trust your skill and try than not try at all. The more you trust your skill the better you will be at it, even with all the failures that await you.

True grit will get you through this process, and once you are on the other side, peak performance awaits you. Trust leads to confidence, but confidence can be a problem if we don't remain students. Just being confident doesn't mean you've attained mastery. On the contrary, confidence can lead to arrogance, and this is what separates an individual who is competent at their skill from a master.

8

BECOME A MASTER, LIVE YOUR LEGEND

Cultivating skill and reaching peak performance leads you to become the master you were meant to be. A master is not arrogantly confident, but rather *radically humble*. When we become arrogant because we "think" we are the best at what we do, life will have a way of knocking us off our pedestal. If you've become arrogant in your skill, then you haven't truly learned anything from the process.

Sincerely learning any skill is ironically a tool for reducing our ego. All of the trials and tribulations should humble your ego, not enhance it. And if you have become egotistical, then it is time to pause and reflect. Being cocky is not a virtue, no matter how much you are paid for being so. Cockiness is not the trait of a master, even if you are highly skillful. Arrogantly confident people might be great at what they do, but they will never be legends. Legendary status is isolated to those who learned life lessons through their skill. To become a master is to attain the qualities of one. A world-class performer strives to reach this level of mastery.

Being Legendary

A master of a skill is a legend in their field, and they leave behind a legacy. Very few people reach this state of mastery. They are the ones willing to suffer and sacrifice to go *all the way*. A master's skill becomes a tool for exploring their inmost nature. Their goals of reaching their optimal potential keep them grounded and sharp, still willing to learn even if they are considered to be at the top of their game. Their skill has given them everything to be a natural human being.

In martial arts the skills learned from the master are not just techniques, but more importantly life lessons. And while our actual skills may differ, the life skills we learn from our respective disciplines are similar. Reaching our optimal potential is dependent on how we act in all facets of life.

Attaining mastery relies on your skill transforming your character. Actually cultivating skill, if done right, trains our character to be virtuous, which has lasting effects. Learning any skill invariably requires you to defer to someone more experienced. Deference teaches humility, respect, compassion, and honor. These in turn teach you to be *radically honest*, even conscious of white lies we tell every day. It is hard for a master to sense when you are lying at all times, so it is up to you to train yourself to be radically honest. But make sure your honesty is not related to subjective opinions, which many people believe is being honest.

The practice of being 100 percent honest is focused on realizing how much we lie to others and ourselves, including those supposedly innocuous white lies. This trains us to be truthful, and as a result people can trust us. An honest mind comes from a humble heart. And humility is the core virtue behind our life skills. The act of deference itself trains us to be humble.

In the modern world we don't like anyone telling us what to do, even if someone is more knowledgeable than we are. We always want to save face and appear as a know-it-all. But a true master remains humble even when they are considered a legend. They reach such an optimal state by continually admitting that they really don't know anything. They embody the seeker's mind. And they were perfectly comfortable bowing to the master before them. By taking the low road they gained all the power necessary to succeed.

Humility attained from learning a skill from a master becomes the bedrock of our character. Respect, honor, compassion, forgiveness, and honesty depend on the humility deep in our heart. But the low road to humility is not all smooth sailing. To defer to a master to learn a skill doesn't mean they have to be particularly nice. One of the reasons people don't reach their full potential is that their common acquaintances are people who tell them what they think they *want* to hear as opposed to what they *need* to hear.

We've all been children who were interested in a skill, but when we began to learn it we resented the teacher because all of the flowery pleasantries and boosting of our ego had been replaced with the reality of hard work and dedication. And the reality is that most kids don't know much about what they are trying to learn, though when we are kids we think we know it all. We all want everything for free and everyone to stroke our ego, but that is an illusionary world full of angels and unicorns. If you are not willing to accept the harsh fact of reality that you don't know much and that there are a lot of people out there better at your chosen skill than you, then mastery will elude you.

A master will dent your ego on purpose for two reasons: (1) they know what is best for you and (2) they've been in your shoes, so they know how to get you to where they are. They know how to counter all the negative reactions one has when one defers to a master. When we are too rebellious they humiliate our childish attitude; when we are too lippy their sharp wit destroys a counterargument; and so on.

The film *Kill Bill: Volume 2* is a great example of this process of a student deferring to a master. In the film, Beatrix Kiddo (played by Uma Thurman) is sent by her fiancé Bill (played by David Carradine) to train in isolation with a master named Pai Mei (played by Gordon

Liu). Pai Mei is a martial arts master specializing in the Bak Mei style of kung fu. The location is an ideal setting similar to the mystical landscape in Chinese nature art. From the outset Pai Mei tests Kiddo. She is training in martial arts essentially to become an assassin. At the beginning of her training she continually fails, and Pai Mei shows her extreme contempt. Nothing Kiddo does is ever good enough for Pai Mei; he wants more.

After a grueling day of training, which involved Kiddo repeatedly practicing a one-inch punch on wood, leaving no skin on her knuckles; she is finding it hard to eat her rice with chopsticks because her hands are so banged up. She throws the chopsticks down to the floor and starts eating with her hands. This infuriates Pai Mei, and he empties her bowl on the ground and tells her that if she wants to eat like a dog, then she can live and sleep outside like a dog. He then gets her a new bowl of rice and tells her that if she wants to live and sleep like a human, then she should pick up her chopsticks. She does and begins to eat with her chopsticks, which makes Pai Mei extremely happy. Pai Mei is one tough son of a bitch, but Kiddo is learning immeasurable lessons that will forge her own path to mastery. Life lessons and skillful training are often learned from teachers who are stern, but the irony is that students often develop a love and respect for the teacher for treating them this way. A real master doesn't sugarcoat things.

If you want to forge your own path to mastery, this sort of process cannot be skipped (though it might not be as extreme as it was for Kiddo). To be a legend you have to endure all of the ups and downs on your way to mastery. The stern discipline Pai Mei showed toward Kiddo gave her skill and transformed her character. She learned the deep lessons of humility, patience, mindfulness, and so on, which in turn trained her speech, thoughts, and actions.

This training of speech, thoughts, and actions is the central moral tenet in the noble eightfold path of the Buddha, who taught such a system because it leads to the mastery of self, reducing the influence of our self-interested and self-centered ego. Skill inadvertently trains our character, which also effects our speech, thoughts, and actions. A legend is mindful of all three of these elements and, as a result, is an admirable role model for others.

Mastery not only means you have reached your peak performance in your skill, but also that your character has become harmonious with the world. You move through the world following your heart's desires without feeling attached or bound by anything, in much the same way Confucius felt at seventy years old. A legend's legacy lives on to teach the world, as we still feel the teachings of masters such as Buddha and Confucius today.

Wisdom

In this book, I've focused on the very real possibility that you can reach your full potential. But where to after that? To live your legend means you must lead by example. Once you have mastery over yourself, you will yearn to pass it on to others. A master who shares their skill and wisdom with others is not only good for students but also teaches the master more about the virtue of humility, respect, selfless care, and so on. The act of teaching itself inculcates compassion and patience.

Wisdom is dependent on true understanding and our ability to pass it onto others. But to do so means we have embodied everything I put forth in this book, from understanding the science of skill and peak performance to training ourselves to downregulate cold cognition to allow our ingrained nature to bring inspiration to the world. Achieving peak performance transforms your inmost nature. Following the four fundamentals and a strict schedule for deep work gives you much needed discipline. That discipline gets you out of your head and into your heart, meaning out of the analytical mind of cold cognition and back into the holistic mind of hot cognition.

A master cannot teach if their wisdom is based on subjective beliefs and opinions wound up in their personality. Their wisdom must be spontaneously natural. Mastery requires that we don't overthink.

Wisdom is beyond overthinking. To reach peak performance and also pass on wisdom we have to come in contact with the naked self beneath our personality. The king with no armor.

Our spontaneous wisdom arises from that naturally pure side of our mind, deep down in the hot system. The continual practice of meditation dissolves ever so slowly the masks we've been hiding behind. This is the process of downregulating cold cognition, so we can peer into our true nature. Most people in the world never get to know their naked, maskless self. A master is intimate with this naked self and knows that a person's optimal potential is dependent on it.

The great South Korean mountain climber Um Hong-gil is one such master. He climbed the fourteen eight-thousand meter peaks in the world. His goal was to accomplish this in twelve years. He climbed to the summit of all fourteen within twelve years, reaching his goal. Hong-gil climbed a few of the mountains more than once, including standing on top of Mount Everest three times. His feats are truly amazing. Many aspiring mountain climbers in South Korea were trained under his tutelage. And just like Pai Mei, he was stern and honest with his students. He had to be because mountain climbing is no joke. It can be fatal, so it isn't for the fainthearted. Eventually a doctor advised Hong-gil to retire because of a leg injury he sustained from years of mountain climbing. But Hong-gil did not listen and continued to follow his passion. In a scene in the film *The Himalayas*, Hong-gil (played by Hwang Jung-min) is on a radio broadcast, and he is asked to share some of the insights he learned from mountain climbing. His response is profound:

From 7,000 meters it seems like you'll learn to live your life. If you go up to 8,000 meters, it seems like you'll discover the meaning of life. But up there, you'll never discover such things. The only thing you can feel up there is yourself. When you're so exhausted and desperate, the real you emerges. All the masks you've been using fall away. Most people never get to know their own unmasked face.[1]

Pushing yourself to reach your optimal potential reveals your unmasked face. A master's role is to push you to the point of exhaustion and frustration. At that point of desperation you learn the most about yourself. In that place you are completely present; no problem in the world moves you. This state of consciousness is the essence of mastery. Your mind has completely fasted away the "person" within you who suffers, and as a result your spontaneous nature takes over and functions in harmony with nature. In losing your grip on yourself, you become who you truly are beneath the veneer of persona. To be a master you need to know how to go beyond yourself to serve something greater. Mastery depends on transcending yourself in selfless service to the world.

In Service to Something Greater Than Yourself

The continual cultivation of skill will thin out your character. An optimal experience depends on it. The more "you" are out of the way, the more you will serve the world selflessly. This does not mean you will serve the world in a voluntary manner. On the contrary, after years or decades of discipline you become absorbed in your skill, which in turn serves the world in its own unique way. Your small piece contributes to the greater whole, piece by piece. As primatologist, ethologist, and anthropologist Jane Goodall once said:

> We hear think globally, act locally. Don't. If you think globally you'll become filled with gloom. But if you take a little piece of this whole picture, my piece, our piece, this is what I can do here, I'm making a difference. And wow, they're making a difference over there and so are they and so are they. And so gradually the pieces get filled in and the world is a better place because of you.[2]

We may not all be Gandhi, but you are you, and you have the kernel of inspiration wound up inside you crying to be free.

Optimization is experienced when we have absorbed ourselves in our skill; intelligent spontaneity guarantees that. Optimization is a state of consciousness experienced when the cold cognition has downregulated. Our life is optimal when we have transcended the boundaries of self. As a result our life is about something greater than ourselves. Being absorbed in something greater than yourself, such as a skill or cause, serves the world in immeasurable ways.

Self-preservation becomes secondary to a feeling of connection with life. That feeling of connection is experienced when the cold system has downregulated to allow the natural hot system to move in unison with life. Our world centered on cold cognitive training has taken onboard an abstract rationality. A mind focused on rationality destroys this sense of connection. Rationality strengthens the illusion of not only minds separate from bodies, but also a self separate from life. We *are* life. We are mind-body integrated organisms that are part of a much larger organism of nature. We are not truthfully calculated self-centered creatures struggling in conflict with life. That is only what we are trained to believe.

What we actually are is heart-centered, in connection with life itself. Though our hot intuitions can be wrong, they invariably give us this sense of connection we have naturally in our hot system. Mencius, the ancient Chinese sage, explained this by coming to the conclusion that our true nature is fundamentally good. This was Lao-tzu's view as well, though the two perspectives differ somewhat.

Mencius illustrates our innate goodness using two metaphors. The first is a story of Ox Mountain. In the story, Mencius and a student are debating over whether human nature is fundamentally good. The student is talking about the mountains in the area, all of which are lush and green except for Ox Mountain, which is barren and desolate. The student's point is that because Ox Mountain is desolate, its nature is fundamentally bad. Mencius's counter argument reveals a glaring fact that the student overlooked. Mencius points out the close proximity of Ox Mountain to a large country:

The woods on Ox Mountain were once beautiful! On account of its being on the edge of a large country, it had been attacked with axes and hatchets, and then how could it remain beautiful? The refreshing breezes of day and night, and the moisture provided by rain and fog, did not fail to give rise to sprouts of vegetation. But cows and sheep have been repeatedly pastured there, and for that reason it has remained desolate. People observe its denuded state and assume that it never had any good resources. But how could this state be the true nature of this mountain?[3]

Ox Mountain's nature was not fundamentally bad; it was the environment that surrounded it that was toxic. All of those years on the edge of a large country made it appear toxic externally, but internally the sprouts continued to grow. Mencius's point is that Ox Mountain is a metaphor for how human beings truly are within. So "bad" people are not innately bad; they are just products of toxic environments that shift their innate goodness in a different direction, essentially warping their nature.

His second metaphor also articulates this point. He uses a story of a child fetching water from a well to evoke this innate sense of goodness within all of us.

Picture yourself in this story as a bystander. You watch a child go to the well to retrieve water. The weight of the bucket is too heavy, and the child is about to fall in the well. What would your instinctual reaction be? Most of us would do anything humanly possible to stop the child from falling. That instinctual response is our natural hot cognition beneath the rationality of cold cognition. In such a situation there is no time for rationality. The situation requires a spontaneous response, and our spontaneous response, as Mencius points out, is naturally good. We'll do anything to save the child. We are just hardwired that way.

What the child-and-well story illustrates is that our innate goodness connects us to the world in a harmonious way. We serve something greater than ourselves when "we" get out of the way of nature.

An optimal experience depends on this formula. World-class performers have this particular knack for selfless service. Sacrificing their time for discipline in their skill while helping others, serves the world. And while their aggressive drive and entrepreneurial spirit are alive and well, they are not self-interested, as they know their life amounts to connection with the world, and so they seek to connect and inspire. Optimizing your life reveals your innate goodness to be brave for others in a world lacking heroes. In the child-and-well story, a true hero throws self-preservation out the door to serve another.

The Brave Hero

A brave person will go to extreme lengths to serve a world in dire need of heroes. Our commitment to discipline in both skill and lifestyle is the choice we need to make to be a hero. A hero is selfless, brave, humble, and forever growing. Their life is in service to their skill, and that skill inspires the world. A hero is a fountain of inspiration. A hero is willing to push the limits and go beyond common expectation; this is true bravery. Bravery at all costs is an optimal state. Going to whatever lengths are necessary to do your best in accord with what is right is bravery. A brave hero pushes normal expectations of what is possible.

A great example of fearless bravery is Baek Jun-ho, another South Korean mountain climber. Jun-ho, a student of the master mountain climber Um Hong-gil mentioned earlier, was part of an expedition to climb Mount Everest, led by Hong-gil's star pupil Park Moo-taek. Jun-ho and Moo-taek were old friends. They had met at university and coincidently met Hong-gil on the Kangchenjunga mountain many years before becoming experienced climbers.

Moo-taek and his schoolmates organized a climb on Mount Everest. They arrived in Nepal with Hong-gil, but he went his own way to climb Gyachung Kang. Once they were established at the Everest basecamp, Moo-taek set out with his team to climb to the summit. They reached the top, but on the way back down Moo-taek and his team encountered bad weather, and as a result Jang Min, another of the team members, became exhausted and started slowing down. Moo-taek's role as team captain was to make sure everybody was safe, so he told the rest of the team to continue without them. But Moo-taek started to go snow blind while he was waiting for Min to recuperate, so he sent Min down by himself because he couldn't see. Min said he would get help once he arrived back at basecamp. Nobody was to see Min ever again.

Moo-taek was effectively trapped high up on Everest, and he was in a lot of pain because he was running out of oxygen. He radioed Jun-ho explaining the situation. Many teams from different countries wanted to help, but the sun was setting, and the majority of them would not go up because it was too dangerous. One Italian team did set out to find Moo-taek, but the terrible weather forced them to come back down. Jun-ho then sent up an experienced Nepalese Sherpa named Nima. Nima set out to rescue Moo-taek, but he too soon came back down because he was frightened of being in such horrible weather in the dark (as we all would be).

Other expedition teams told Jun-ho to forget about Moo-taek, saying it was too late. But Jun-ho did not listen and did one of the bravest things someone has ever done. At just after 6:00 p.m. he walked fearlessly in the freezing cold dark of night to find his friend. Although Nima followed him for a bit, he eventually returned to the camp, and Jun-ho continued on fearlessly through the pitch black dark of night. Amazingly Jun-ho radioed basecamp at 6:00 a.m., saying that he had found Moo-taek. The Korean team at basecamp urged Jun-ho to bring Moo-taek back down, but it was too late. Jun-ho explained that Moo-taek already had second degree frostbite, and it would soon become third degree, which meant that death was imminent. Jun-ho's last words to basecamp were, "Eight thousand, seven hundred meters high; rescuing Moo-taek is impossible." Tragically, Jun-ho never returned. Did he know he was going to die? It probably didn't matter. Finding his friend was what mattered most to him; it was more important than his own life. Jun-ho didn't want his friend to die alone. This is heroism and bravery at a level most of us are not ready for. Nature got the best of Jun-ho and Moo-taek, but it was Jun-ho's courage that will be part of legend.

There is a second part to this story, and it involves Um Hong-gil. After the deaths of Jun-ho and Moo-taek, Hong-gil was devastated and wanted to bring them both home to South Korea. Although the chances of finding either of them were slim, he established a team of experienced climbers, some of whom were old friends, and the team made the journey up above 8000 meters. It was like finding a needle in a hay stack, but they finally found Moo-taek, who was frozen solid.

When Hong-gil greeted his friend it was one of the most moving events you'll ever see (watch the real-life event in the Korean MBC documentary *Ah! Everest* or the film *The Himalayas*). They never found Jun-ho, though they tried (they accidentally found another climber frozen solid). They attempted to bring Moo-taek back to the Everest basecamp, and though the team did their best, they struggled with the heavy weight of Moo-taek's frozen body. Hong-gil didn't want to give up, but the task became increasingly difficult, and he finally had to make the heartbreaking call to leave Moo-taek on the mountain. It seemed as if Moo-taek didn't want to leave, and he belongs to the mountain now.

The team gave Moo-taek a proper burial with stones high up on Mount Everest. Both Moo-taek and Jun-ho belong to the great mountain, but their lives have become legend. And Hong-gil's courage to find his friends is the type of heroism we need to reach our full potential. This does not mean you need to go crazy and try to climb Mount Everest (unless that is your desire). These two stories show us the type of courage we need to persevere with our skill. If we want to reach our optimal potential we cannot give up. We must stay strong and embody the heroic heart of Jun-ho: fearless in life and a friend you can count on. What length will you go to live your legend?

Peak Performance

Everything in this book is designed to help you to be the best version of yourself. The science and strategies explained are the necessary fuel for your greatness. Come to understand the ancient and modern methods for comprehending the embodied mind, meaning the mind is embodied and the body is mindful. Use the two-system model to better understand how to develop skill and reach peak performance. Apply the training methods described in this book and remain committed to them. That discipline will surely take your life to the next level.

A peak-performance lifestyle depends on nourishing the four fundamentals: meditation, nutrition, exercise, and sleep. Once that bedrock is firm, your life will grow. Your skill will flower, and your peak state of performance will inspire the world. It's just a matter of committing to living the life you were born to live. It's time to actualize your full potential. What are you waiting for?

NOTES

Introduction.
The Formula for Expert Skill
and Peak Performance

1. Campbell, *Power of Myth*, 4–5.

1. The Embodied Mind

1. Kahneman, *Thinking, Fast and Slow*, 11.
2. Kahneman, *Thinking, Fast and Slow*, 11.
3. Huxley, *Perennial Philosophy*, 141.
4. Kahneman, *Thinking, Fast and Slow*, 35.

2. Intelligent Spontaneity

1. Chuang Tzu, *Complete Works*, 50–51.
2. Slingerland, *Trying Not to Try*, 29.

3. Discipline and Structure

1. Confucius, *Analects*, 9.
2. Capra, *Tao of Physics*, 124.

4. The Four Fundamentals

1. Sadhguru, "How to Get Rid of Stress," Sadhguru (website).

2. Slingerland, *Trying Not to Try,* 28.
3. David Perlmutter, "How Can Eating Gluten Affect the Health of My Brain?" davidperlmutter MD (website).
4. David Perlmutter, "Preventing Alzheimer's and Other Brain Illnesses," davidperlmutter MD (website).
5. Kelly, *The Yin and Yang of Climate Crisis,* 54–55.
6. Ferriss, *Tools of Titans,* 28.
7. Ferriss, *Tools of Titans,* 65.
8. Tom Rath, *Eat Move Sleep,* 61–62.
9. "Will 10,000 Steps a Day Make You Fit?" Peak Fitness (website).
10. David Bassett Jr. et al., "Pedometer-Measured Physical Activity and Health Behaviors in U.S. Adults," *Medicine & Science in Sports & Exercise,* 42, no. 10 (October 2010), 1819–25.
11. Ferriss, *Tools of Titans,* 70.
12. National Strength and Conditioning Association, *Essentials of Strength Training and Conditioning,* 512–13.
13. Arne Dietrich, "Functional Neuroanatomy of Altered States of Consciousness: The Transient Hypofrontality Hypothesis," *Consciousness and Cognition* 12, no. 2 (June 2003), 231–56.
14. Walker, *Why We Sleep,* 137.
15. Walker, *Why We Sleep,* 3.
16. Walker, *Why We Sleep,* 107.
17. M. P. St-Onge, A. Roberts, A. Shechter, and A. R. Choudhury, "Fiber and Saturated Fat Are Associated with Sleep Arousals and Slow Wave Sleep," *Journal of Clinical Sleep Medicine* 12 (2016): 19–24.

5. Cultivate Intelligence and Harness Creativity

1. Krishnamurti, *Krishnamurti on Education,* 57.
2. Ferriss, *Tools of Titans,* 484.
3. Cal Newport, *Deep Work,* 3.

6. Fasting the Mind

1. Chuang Tzu, *Complete Works,* 57–58.
2. Slingerland, *Trying Not to Try,* 161–62.
3. Richard E. Nisbett, *The Geography of Thought,* 34–35.
4. Petter Neby, "About Us," Punkt. (website).

5. Giovanna Dunmall, "Smartphone Backlash: The Mobile That Gives You Your Life Back," Guardian (website), February 22, 2018.

6. Wikipedia, s.v. "negativity bias."

7. The Nature of Peak Performance

1. PursueFitnessTV, *Tony Ferguson UFC 209 | In The Zone,* February 17, 2017, YouTube video.

2. Watts, *Become What You Are,* 114.

8. Become a Master, Live Your Legend

1. *The Himalayas,* directed by Lee Seok-hoon, featuring Hwang Jung-min, Jung Woo, and Jo Sung-ha, released December 16, 2015.

2. National Geographic, "Jane Goodall: Hero—Tribute to Dr. Goodall for Her 80th Birthday in 2014," National Geographic YouTube channel, October 28, 2016.

3. Wikipedia, s.v. "Ox Mountain."

BIBLIOGRAPHY

Austin, James. *Zen and the Brain*. Cambridge, Mass.: MIT Press, 1999.

Beilock, Sian. *Choke*. New York: Free Press, 2010.

Benoit, Hubert. *Zen and the Psychology of Transformation*. Rochester, Vt.: Inner Traditions, 1990.

Blofeld, John. *Taoism: Road to Immortality*. Boston: Shambhala, 2000.

Campbell, Joseph. *Myths of Light*. Novato, Calif.: New World Library, 2003.

———. *Pathways to Bliss*. Novato, Calif.: New World Library, 2004.

———. *The Power of Myth*. New York: Anchor Books, 1991.

Capra, Fritjof. *The Tao of Physics*. Boston: Shambhala, 2000.

Chuang Tsu. *Chuang Tsu: Inner Chapters; A Companion Volume to Tao Te Ching*. Translated by Gia-Fu Feng and Jane English. Portland, Oreg.: Amber Lotus, 2008.

Chuang Tzu. *The Complete Works of Chuang Tzu*. Translated by Burton Watson. New York: Columbia University Press, 1968.

Clark, Andy. *Being There: Putting Brain, Body, and World Together Again*. Cambridge, Mass.: A Bradford Book, 1997.

Cleary, Thomas. *The Taoism Reader*. Boston: Shambhala, 2012.

Confucius. *Analects*. Translated by Edward Slingerland. Indianapolis, Ind.: Hackett Publishing, 2003.

Csikszentmihalyi, Mihaly. *Flow*. New York: Harper and Row, 1990.

Dennett, Daniel. *Consciousness Explained*. Boston: Back Bay Books, 1991.

Dietrich, Arne. *Introduction to Consciousness*. London: Palgrave Macmillan, 2007.

Durkheim, Emile. *The Elementary Forms of Religious Life*. New York: Oxford University Press, 2008.

Dyer, Wayne W. *Wisdom of the Ages: 60 Days to Enlightenment*. New York: William Morrow, 2002.

Easwaran, Eknath, trans. *The Upanishads*. Tomales, Calif.: Nilgiri Press, 2007.

Ferriss, Tim. *Tools of Titans*. New York: Houghton Mifflin Harcourt, 2017.

Flanagan, Owen. *The Bodhisattva's Brain*. Cambridge, Mass.: A Bradford Book, 2013.

Godman, David. *Be as You Are: The Teaching of Sri Ramana Maharshi*. Delhi, India: Penguin Books, 1992.

Gregory, Jason. *Effortless Living*. Rochester, Vt.: Inner Traditions, 2018.

———. *Enlightenment Now*. Rochester, Vt.: Inner Traditions, 2016.

———. *Fasting the Mind*. Rochester, Vt.: Inner Traditions, 2017.

———. *The Science and Practice of Humility*. Rochester, Vt.: Inner Traditions, 2014.

Griffith, Ralph T. H. *The Hymns of the Rgveda*. Delhi, India: Motilal Banarsidass Publishers, 1999.

Guenon, Rene. *The Essential Rene Guenon*. Bloomington, Ind.: World Wisdom, Inc., 2009.

Hanh, Thich Nhat. *Silence*. London: Rider, 2015.

Hanson, Rick. *Buddha's Brain*. Oakland, Calif.: New Harbinger Publications Inc., 2009.

Hart, William. *The Art of Living: Vipassana Meditation*. New York: Harper One, 1987.

Holiday, Ryan. *Ego Is the Enemy*. New York: Portfolio, 2016.

———. *The Obstacle Is the Way*. New York: Portfolio, 2014.

Holman, John. *The Return of the Perennial Philosophy*. London: Watkins, 2008.

Huxley, Aldous. *The Perennial Philosophy*. New York: Harper Perennial Modern Classics, 2009.

Ivanhoe, Philip J. *The Daodejing of Laozi*. Indianapolis, Ind.: Hackett Publishing Company, 2003.

Ivanhoe, Philip J., and Bryan W. Van Norden. *Readings in Classical Chinese Philosophy*. Indianapolis, Ind.: Hackett Publishing Company, 2005.

Kahneman, Daniel. *Thinking, Fast and Slow*. London: Penguin, 2012.

Kelly, Brendan. *The Yin and Yang of Climate Crisis: Healing Personal, Cultural, and Ecological Imbalance with Chinese Medicine.* Berkeley, Calif.: North Atlantic Books, 2015.

Kingsley, Peter. *Reality.* Point Reyes, Calif.: The Golden Sufi Center, 2004.

Krishnamurti, Jiddu. *Krishnamurti on Education.* Krishnamurti Foundation India, 2012.

———. *Krishnamurti: Reflections on the Self.* Chicago, Ill.: Open Court, 1998.

———. *Total Freedom.* New York: Harper One, 1996.

Lao-tzu. *Tao Te Ching: An Illustrated Journey.* Translated by Stephen Mitchell. London: Frances Lincoln, 2009.

Maharshi, Sri Ramana. *Saddarsanam and An Inquiry into the Revelation of Truth and Oneself.* Translated by Nome. Santa Cruz, Calif: Society of Abidance in Truth, 2009.

Masters, Robert Augustus. *Spiritual Bypassing.* Berkeley, Calif.: North Atlantic Books, 2010.

Mengzi. *Mengzi.* Translated by Bryan W. Van Norden. Indianapolis, Ind.: Hackett Publishing, 2008.

Merton, Thomas. *The Way of Chuang Tzu.* New York: New Directions, 2010.

National Strength and Conditioning Association. *Essentials of Strength Training and Conditioning.* 3rd ed. Champaign, Ill.: Human Kinetics, 2008.

Newport, Cal. *Deep Work: Rules for Focused Success in a Distracted World.* New York: Grand Central Publishing, 2016.

Nisbett, Richard E. *The Geography of Thought: How Asians and Westerners Think Differently . . . and Why.* New York: Free Press, 2003.

Olivelle, Patrick. *Upanishads.* New York: Oxford University Press, 1996.

Ouspensky, P. D. *In Search of the Miraculous: The Teachings of G. I. Gurdjieff.* Orlando, Fla.: Harcourt, 2001.

Patanjali. *The Yoga-Sutra of Patanjali: A New Translation with Commentary.* Translated by Chip Hartranft. Boston: Shambhala, 2003.

Perlmutter, David. *Brain Maker.* New York: Little, Brown and Company, 2015.

———. *Grain Brain: The Surprising Truth about Wheat, Carbs, and Sugar; Your Brain's Silent Killers.* New York: Little, Brown and Company, 2013.

———. *The Grain Brain Whole Life Plan: Boost Brain Performance, Lose Weight, and Achieve Optimal Health.* New York: Little, Brown and Company, 2016.

Pine, Red. *The Heart Sutra.* Berkeley, Calif.: Counterpoint, 2005.

———. *The Zen Teachings of Bodhidharma.* Berkeley, Calif.: North Point Press, 1989.

Pinker, Steven. *How the Mind Works*. New York: W. W. Norton and Company Inc., 1997.

———. *The Language Instinct: How the Mind Creates Language*. New York: Harper Perennial Modern Classics, 2007.

Radhakrishnan, Sarvepalli. *The Bhagavadgita*. Noida, India: Harper Collins India, 2010.

Rath, Tom. *Eat Move Sleep: How Small Choices Lead to Big Changes*. Missionday, 2013.

Schuon, Frithjof. *The Transcendent Unity of Religions*. Wheaton, Ill.: Quest Books, 1984.

Shankara. *Shankara's Crest Jewel of Discrimination*. Translated by Swami Prabhavananda and Christopher Isherwood. Los Angeles: Vedanta Society of Southern California, 1975.

Slingerland, Edward. *Trying Not to Try: The Art and Science of Spontaneity*. New York: Broadway Books, 2014.

Slingerland, Edward, and Mark Collard. *Creating Consilience: Integrating the Sciences and the Humanities*. New York: Oxford, 2012.

Suzuki, Daisetz Teitaro, trans. *The Lankavatara Sutra: A Mahayana Text*. Philadelphia: Coronet Books, 1999.

Suzuki, Shunryu. *Zen Mind, Beginner's Mind: Informal Talks on Zen Meditation and Practice*. Boston: Shambhala, 2011.

Walker, Matthew. *Why We Sleep*. London: Penguin, 2018.

Watts, Alan. *Become What You Are*. Boston: Shambhala, 2003.

———. *The Book*. New York: Vintage Books, 1989.

———. *Do You Do It, or Does It Do You: How to Let the Universe Meditate You*. Louisville, Colo.: Sounds True, 2005. Audio CD.

———. *Out of Your Mind: Essential Listening from the Alan Watts Audio Archives*. Louisville, Colo.: Sounds True, 2004. Audio CD.

———. *Tao: The Watercourse Way*. New York: Pantheon, 1977.

———. *The Way of Zen*. New York: Vintage Books, 1999.

———. *The Wisdom of Insecurity*. New York: Vintage Books, 2011.

Welwood, John. *Perfect Love, Imperfect Relationships: Healing the Wound of the Heart*. Boston: Trumpeter, 2007.

———. *Toward a Psychology of Awakening: Buddhism, Psychotherapy, and the Path of Personal and Spiritual Transformation*. Boston: Shambhala, 2002.

Wilhelm, Richard. *The I Ching, or Book of Changes*. Princeton, N.J.: Princeton University Press, 1967.

———. *The Secret of the Golden Flower: A Chinese Book of Life*. London: Arkana, 1984.

Xunzi. *Xunzi*. Translated by Burton Watson. New York: Columbia University Press, 2003.

INDEX

Page numbers in *italics* indicate illustrations.

Books of Related Interest

Effortless Living
Wu-Wei and the Spontaneous State of Natural Harmony
by Jason Gregory
Foreword by Damo Mitchell

Fasting the Mind
Spiritual Exercises for Psychic Detox
by Jason Gregory

Enlightenment Now
Liberation Is Your True Nature
by Jason Gregory

The Science and Practice of Humility
The Path to Ultimate Freedom
by Jason Gregory
Foreword by Daniel Reid

Being Present
Cultivate a Peaceful Mind through Spiritual Practice
by Darren Cockburn

Awakening the Chakras
The Seven Energy Centers in Your Daily Life
by Victor Daniels, Kooch N. Daniels, and Pieter Weltevrede

The Yoga-Sutra of Patañjali
A New Translation and Commentary
by Georg Feuerstein, Ph.D.

Healing Love through the Tao
Cultivating Female Sexual Energy
by Mantak Chia

Healing Light of the Tao
Foundational Practices to Awaken Chi Energy
by Mantak Chia

INNER TRADITIONS • BEAR & COMPANY
P.O. Box 388 • Rochester, VT 05767
1-800-246-8648 • www.InnerTraditions.com

Or contact your local bookseller